JAPANESE AMERICANS ANI

Japanese Americans and World War II

Mass Removal, Imprisonment, and Redress

FOURTH EDITION

Donald Teruo Hata
and
Nadine Ishitani Hata

Harlan Davidson, Inc.
Wheeling, Illinois 60090-6000

Library of Congress Cataloging-in-Publication Data

Hata, Donald Teruo, 1939–
 Japanese Americans and World War II : mass removal, imprisonment,
and redress / Donald Teruo Hata and Nadine Ishitani Hata. — 4th ed.
     p. cm.
 Includes bibliographical references and index.
 ISBN 978-0-88295-279-6 (alk. paper)
1. Japanese Americans—Evacuation and relocation, 1942–1945.
2. World War, 1939–1945—Evacuation of civilians—United States.
3. Concentration camps—United States. 4. Japanese Americans—Civil
rights. 5. Japanese Americans—Reparations. I. Hata, Nadine Ishitani.
II. Title.
 D769.8.A6H37 2011
 940.53'17089956073—dc22

                                                     2010041809

On the cover: Hatsuko Mary Higuchi, *Executive Order 9066, Series 4*,
watercolor on paper, 30 inches by 22 inches, Collection of the artist.
Email: maryhiguchiarts@yahoo.com
Cover design: Linda Gaio

Manufactured in the United States of America
14 13 12 11 1 2 3 4 MG

In memory of
Nadine Ishitani Hata
March 15, 1941–February 25, 2005

Contents

Map, Documents (Executive Order 9066, and Instructions to implement Civilian Exclusion Order No. 108), and Photographs follow page 56

Preface and
Acknowledgments

Like its predecessors, the first of which was published in 1974, this fourth edition of Japanese Americans and World War II is intended as a succinct and affordable supplement to history and political science texts that minimize or neglect the Nikkei (Japanese American) experience in World War II. As was hoped, the first two editions of this publication found an enthusiastic reception by instructors and students alike at the high school, community college, and university level. In addition, the expanded third edition found a new readership beyond the classroom, in members of and visitors to museums, such as the Japanese American Museum in Los Angeles, and interpretive centers at former concentration camp sites administered by the National Park Service at Manzanar, Tule Lake, and others in progress.

In response to the supportive and constructive feedback of students, instructors, and lay readers of all walks of life, the staff at Harlan Davidson, Inc., and I undertook a bold and sweeping redesign of the third edition that saw the well-loved little "pamphlet" become an attractive but still highly affordable book that, in addition to taking the narrative completely up to date, has been thoroughly re-edited and expanded further to include photographs, key documents, and an enhanced multidisciplinary bibliography of 200 core publications by historians, political scientists, sociologists, anthropologists, and others, as well as multimedia and Internet-based sources. Inaccurate and misleading euphemisms such as "evacuation" and "imprisonment" have been meticulously replaced with more accurate terms like "mass removal" and "imprisonment— changes explained and amplified in a new "Note on Terminology," which explains the movement to correct long out-dated language and refers readers to thoughtful essays on the subject by eminent scholars.

Barbara Takei and the late Jack Herzig assisted me in making critical revisions incorporated in this fourth edition. Especially helpful, however, were the efforts of Aiko Herzig-Yoshinaga, to whom I owe a debt of gratitude. A continuous infusion of information, constructive criticisms, and recommendations over the past four decades has also come from students, colleagues, mentors, government officials, and community activists, but any errors of fact or interpretation are mine alone. Linda Gaio, also at Harlan Davidson, designed the cover, for which the artist Hatsuko Mary Higuchi graciously permitted us to reproduce one of her works. My sincere thanks to them both. Finally, the publisher Andrew J. Davidson has personally edited every edition save the first, and no author could ask for a more collegial and supportive partner in that role.

—Donald Teruo Hata
Redondo Beach, California

Japanese Americans and World War II

Mass Removal, Imprisonment, and Redress

INTRODUCTION

On February 19, 1942, two months after the United States declared war on Imperial Japan, President Franklin D. Roosevelt issued Executive Order No. 9066. By the summer of 1942, virtually the entire *Nikkei* (Japanese American) population on the U.S. mainland—110,000 men, women, and children—had vanished from their homes, schools, and places of employment in cities and rural communities throughout the coastal areas of the Pacific Coast states. Among the Nikkei who disappeared under U.S. Army guard were 40,000 *Issei* ("first generation" immigrants from Japan) and 70,000 *Nisei* ("second generation"), the American-born sons and daughters of the Issei. Aside from a few neighbors and business acquaintances of the missing persons, most Americans either did not know or chose not to ask why and where the Nikkei had gone. By the end of the year, a vast archipelago of federal concentration camps had been specially constructed and staffed to imprison people whose only "crime" was their Japanese ancestry. Eventually, this inmate population included 6,000 babies born to a birthright of barbed wire and 3,000 Latin American Japanese deportees (of whom 80 percent were from Peru).

Since the end of World War II, the popular American images of Nikkei have changed dramatically, to a degree unimaginable to those who lived through the tumultuous events following the outbreak of the war. In this time the perception of Nikkei has gone from one extreme to another—from sneaky "Yellow Peril" to America's "Model Minority." Former congressman Norman Mineta served as secretary of transportation during the first term of President George W. Bush, and President Barack Obama appointed former U.S. Army chief of staff General Eric Shinseki as secretary of veterans affairs. No less surprising, however, was the success of a Nikkei movement for "redress" undertaken half a century after World War II.

On August 10, 1988, President Ronald Reagan signed the Civil Liberties Act of 1988, which provided each survivor (or eligible heir) of America's World War II concentration camps for Nikkei with a tax-exempt payment of $20,000 and an official apology. Accordingly, on November 21, 1989, Congress approved an annual appropriation to compensate all eligible persons, beginning with the oldest survivors. The first wave of compensatory checks was finally issued on October 9, 1990; they were accompanied by a letter of apology signed by President George H. W. Bush:

A monetary sum and words alone cannot restore lost years or erase painful memories; neither can they fully convey our Nation's resolve to rectify injustice and to uphold the rights of individuals. We can never fully right the wrongs of the past. But we can take a clear stand for justice and recognize that serious injustices were done to Japanese Americans during World War II.

In enacting a law calling for restitution and offering a sincere apology, your fellow Americans have, in a very real sense, renewed their traditional commitment to the ideals of freedom, equality, and justice. You and your family have our best wishes for the future.

What had happened to cause such a shift in attitudes toward Nikkei? Historians of the wartime Nikkei diaspora agree that it was the culmination of a century of intense hostility toward Asian immigrants on the West Coast. An understanding of this explanation requires a brief overview of events prior to the turn of the century.

"Yellow Peril": Issei Pioneers and the Anti-Chinese Legacy

The majority (white) population of the Pacific Coast, and particularly California, where most Japanese immigrants eventually settled, had developed an intense hatred for Chinese long before the arrival of the Issei. By the late 1860s, the Chinese had replaced other groups as the largest colored minority in the Golden State, and vigilante groups and organized labor blamed them for the economic problems of the period. Chinese immigrants soon learned that American laws were enacted, interpreted, and implemented to deny them equal opportunity and equal protection. They were officially classified as "aliens ineligible to citizenship" because federal immigration and naturalization statutes applied only to white and black aliens, and the Chinese were the first foreigners to be singled out by name and prohibited by law from freely entering the United States. The California State Constitution of 1879 denied suffrage to "natives of China." Economic arguments for denying the Chinese U.S. citizenship were augmented by allegations that the Chinese immigrants—typically single young men—gambled, smoked opium, and were unsuitable for acculturation or assimilation in America.

Between 1882 and 1902, Congress passed several Chinese exclusion laws, which would not be relaxed until the middle of World War II. The popular cliche, "you don't have a Chinaman's chance," was a cruel but accurate analogy of the day. By the turn of the century, as Japanese began to arrive to seek their fortunes, the well-entrenched anti-Chinese movement targeted them as the next wave of the "Yellow Peril."

Japanese contract laborers moved to Hawaii as early as 1868, when Japan abandoned its two-centuries-old isolation policy, but very few of the Japanese emigrants settled on the U.S. mainland until the 1890s. The 1880 U.S. census reported a total of 148 Japanese in the country, with 86 in California. Some 3,000 more had arrived by 1890, but most of these were students, merchants, diplomatic officials, and other temporary residents, or "birds of passage" (*dekasegi*). After 1890, however, many Japanese decided to plant permanent roots, and thus emerged the Issei, or "first generation" immigrant pioneers. The census of 1890 counted a total of 2,039 Japanese in America, with 1,147 in California. Within a decade the figure grew to 24,326, of whom more than 10,000 resided in California. The peak period of Issei arrival was between 1900 and 1910, when the national count leaped to 72,157, with California still leading the other states with 41,356. By 1920, the Issei population in California alone approached 72,000, while the national total was 111,000. Due to pressure from the Pacific Coast's majority population to limit Japanese immigration in the 1920s, the 1930 census revealed a significant reduction in the Nikkei population growth: a national total of 138,834, with 97,456 in California.

When these statistics are compared with census figures for the majority population, the numerical insignificance of the Nikkei is dramatic. Even during the peak period of arrival and settlement (1901 to 1910), Nikkei comprised no more than 2 percent of California's total population and barely one-tenth of 1 percent of the total population of the continental United States. Such a tiny minority should have gone unnoticed amidst the vast expanses of California and the rest of the Pacific Coast region. So why all the fuss over so few?

Due to the Chinese exclusion laws, by the early 1890s California faced a critical shortage of laborers and welcomed Issei workers. The newcomers worked for low wages and accepted poor working and living conditions. Members of labor unions, however, saw them as "scabs" who subverted demands for higher pay. In short, the established trade unions were threatened by the entry of Issei into logging, mining, fishing, canneries, and railroad work. In 1903 Japanese and Mexican sugar beet workers in Oxnard, California, formed a unique example of interethnic cooperation when, instead of competing against each other, they organized the Japanese-Mexican Labor Association. Their meetings included simultaneous translations into Spanish, Japanese, and English, and they succeeded in striking for better wages and working conditions. Soon the Japanese immigrants were seen as an even more dangerous version of the "Yellow Peril." On May 14, 1905, delegates from sixty-seven local labor organizations met in San Francisco to form the Asiatic Exclusion League.

THE MOVEMENT FOR JAPANESE EXCLUSION

On October 11, 1906, the San Francisco Board of Education restricted all Japanese and Korean students to one public school that had already been designated for Chinese pupils. In response, the Japanese government issued a strongly worded formal protest and, after the personal intervention of President Theodore Roosevelt, the board rescinded its original order. Roosevelt's defense of the Japanese students in San Francisco inflamed the Exclusion League. Hostility toward Issei immigrants escalated in 1907 when the Native Sons of the Golden West (NSGW), the most influential nativist organization in California, published the first issue of *Grizzly Bear* magazine. A favorite theme of the periodical was Japanese "picture brides" who, according to the NSGW, merely exchanged photographs with their prospective husbands before arriving in America to work as "beasts of burden" seven days a week. Nativists claimed that Japanese immigrants could never be acculturated or assimilated into U.S. society.

By 1908 enterprising Issei like George Shima, the "Potato King" of the Stockton-Sacramento delta in California, had accumulated sufficient savings to purchase their own land. While most Issei were not as successful as Shima and his Empire Delta Farms, which once spanned 6,000 acres, the ability of some Issei to move from farm laborers to farm owners was perceived by nativists as a serious threat to their domination of California agriculture. The rapidly escalating anti-Japanese movement prompted the 1908 "Gentlemen's Agreement," an informal policy whereby Japan unilaterally halted the issuance of passports to Japanese laborers bound for the U.S. mainland. The Japanese government strictly enforced the new policy, causing a major shift of Japanese immigration to destinations in Mexico and Latin America.

The total number of Japanese laborers in the continental United States declined by 30 percent from 1908 to1913, but the entry of thousands of Issei women led to more nativist demands for stronger immigration controls. Now the nativists alleged that Issei families would "breed like rabbits" and inundate the Pacific slope region with children who would be U.S. citizens by birthright. Once those children reached legal maturity, the argument continued, they would pose a dangerous threat to white ownership of land. Pressure mounted for legislation to avoid the future Japanese "takeover," and in 1913 California passed the first of many laws prohibiting "aliens ineligible to citizenship" (i.e., Issei) from either purchasing or leasing land themselves or acting as guardians for the property of their native-born children.

In the meantime, the anti-Japanese movement began to focus on the issue of national security and the questionable loyalty of the Issei and their Nisei children. Japan's surprising victory in the Russo-Japanese War (1904–06) flamed fears concerning the security of the United States' recently acquired colonies in the Philippines and Hawaii. Books and articles of the day demanded that U.S. Navy battleships be assigned permanently to Pacific Coast bases to deter a possible Japanese attack. In 1909, the publication of Homer Lea's *The Valor of Ignorance* created widespread fear that all Japanese

residing in the United States were spies and potential saboteurs for Imperial Japan. The alarmist publication warned
that huge Japanese armies would invade the Pacific Coast and
occupy the western United States to the Rocky Mountains.

National images of Nikkei began to conform to the Pacific Coast stereotype when Wallace Irwin, a San Francisco newspaperman, created a fictitious thirty-five-year-old
Japanese "school-boy" named Hashimoto Togo. Nationally
syndicated cartoons and caricatures of Togo, with his large
buck teeth, portrayed him as always smiling and ingratiating,
nodding while speaking what was perceived as an amusing,
pidgin English. Working in the home of an American family
in order to attend school, Togo secretly planned for the day
when he would use his education against the United States.
As the Togo series appeared in such diverse publications
as the *New York Times* and *Good Housekeeping,* Americans
across the nation became familiar with the stereotype of the
outwardly polite but inwardly sneaky and cunning "Jap."

The anti-Japanese movement seemed to be relegated to
the Pacific Coast during World War I because Japan entered
the conflict on the side of the United States, Great Britain,
and France, but after the war it emerged as part of a national
anti-immigration movement, whose supporters included
some of the most powerful politicians and judges in the
land. In 1922, the U.S. Supreme Court took great care, in the
case of *Takao Ozawa* v. *United States,* to confirm that aliens
of Japanese ancestry were "ineligible to citizenship" via
naturalization because they were neither white nor black.
It made no difference that Ozawa, who petitioned for U.S.
citizenship, had spent most of his life in the United States,
spoke English in his home, graduated from Berkeley High
School, and attended the University of California.

By exploiting the issue of "dual citizenship," exclusionists and xenophobes fed growing national fears that Nikkei, irrespective of U.S. citizenship, were more loyal to Japan than they were to the United States. Like England, France, and many other nations, Japan accepted the code of *jus sanguinis,* under which the children of Japanese were citizens of Japan, regardless of their country of residence or choice. In 1924, Japanese law was revised so that Japan laid claim only to foreign-born children of Japanese parents who were registered in Japan within fourteen days after birth. It is estimated that after 1924, only 20 percent of the Nisei held dual citizenship, but exclusionists continued to use the issue to question the loyalty of the American-born Japanese.

By 1924 the anti-Japanese movement comprised a powerful coalition of racists, nativists, and exclusionists. That year, in concert with an anti-immigration attitude prevalent across the nation, Congress passed an immigration law (the National Origins Act) that set strict quotas on immigrants from nations outside of northwestern Europe; it carried a special provision for the exclusion of Japanese. From 1924 until 1952, when the law was modified, Japanese immigration to the United States virtually ceased.

"200 Percent" American: Emergence of the Nisei

The federal immigration bill of 1924 had such a negative public reception in Japan that many scholars of U.S.-Japanese foreign relations view its passage as one of the first steps in the increasingly inexorable confrontations that led to World War II. For Nikkei, the 1924 law's ban on Japanese immigration had more personal consequences.

The Nisei were U.S. citizens by birthright. Most had never been to Japan. Moreover, like second-generation Americans from Europe, the Nisei tried to mimic the mainstream society. They were "200 percent Americans" who spoke English as their native language and whose contacts with "things Japanese" were limited to the language and cultural traditions practiced by their Issei parents. Japanese first names such as "Takao" or "Kimiko" were modified by young Nisei to "Tak" or "Kimi." The Americanization of Buddhism was already apparent in the holding of Sunday services, by references to "churches" instead of "temples," and by the singing of "Buddha loves me, this I know . . ." to the tune of "Jesus loves me . . . ." Anti-miscegenation laws and restrictive covenants limited social mobility and assimilation, but Nisei attended public schools and interacted with whites; on the eve of World War II, Nisei represented one of the most rapid examples of the acculturation process in United States history.

But in the depressed economic environment of the 1930s, the eagerness of acculturated Nisei to be accepted as Americans was not reciprocated. The nationwide crisis of confidence caused by the Great Depression only exacerbated the racist-nativist need for scapegoats. When it came time to look for jobs and housing, Nisei discovered that they were not full citizens. Nisei college graduates with degrees in architecture or law ended up working in vegetable markets and flower shops. The story of John Aiso, associate justice of the California Court of Appeals, was well known among Nikkei. In 1922, the thirteen-year-old Aiso was elected student body president of Le Conte Junior High School in Hollywood, California. In response to complaints by racist parents, students, and local newspaper stories, the principal abolished student government until Aiso graduated.

During the 1920s and 1930s, Issei parents wondered what kind of future awaited their Nisei children, many of whom were approaching adolescence, for even before the onset of the Depression, the past record promised only cruel and unfair treatment from whites. Some Issei decided to send their children to Japan to become bilingual and bicultural, in case conditions in the United States became intolerable in the future. The young Nisei who were sent to Japan were known as *Kibei* (one who "returns to America"). Many Kibei recall tense relations with "snooty" Nisei "200 percenters" who shunned them for "speaking just-off-the-boat English."

Beside the fact that few could afford the expense, the majority of Issei did not send their children to Japan for an education because they had unreservedly committed themselves to a life in the United States. After all, they reasoned, their chances for upward social and economic mobility— albeit restricted by racist laws and customs—in their new country were still better than they had been under the rigid social class structure and general lack of opportunity that they had left behind in Japan. Thus, they sent their children to local public schools and strongly encouraged academic achievement.

Many Issei parents did send their children to local Japanese language schools in the hope that traditional culture would not be forgotten. Nisei attended the private language schools from early childhood through their high school years, in the afternoons after their regular classes were over and on Saturdays. Many recalled the language classes as a "complete waste of time," with both students and teachers accepting the entire experience as a charade for the Issei parents who were paying the tuition. In fact, during the wartime incarceration, when the U.S. military needed translators, they tested the Japanese-language competency of the Nisei; the results shocked government officials, for the tests revealed that most Nisei could barely read a simple newspaper headline, even after years of attending the Japanese language schools. In the 1930s, however, the anti-Japanese movement attacked the existence of the language schools as evidence that Issei and Nisei were consciously resisting acculturation into the mainstream of American society. Moreover, alleged the alarmists, the language schools were housed in the facilities of "un-American" religions (e.g., Buddhist temples) where a portrait of the Japanese emperor hung instead of, or along with, that of the president of the United States.

As newsreels and newspapers publicized Japan's military aggression and occupation in China throughout the 1930s, most Americans saw little difference between the increasingly ruthless image of Imperial Japan and fellow Americans of Japanese ancestry. Therefore, on the eve of Japan's attack on Pearl Harbor, despite their genuine efforts to assimilate into American culture, the Nikkei lived as strangers in their own land.

War Hysteria, Racism, and Political Expedience

At sunrise on December 7, 1941, without an official declaration of war, aircraft of the Imperial Japanese Navy attacked U.S. military installations at Pearl Harbor, Hawaii. Until the terrorist attacks on New York City and Washington, D.C., on September 11, 2001, "Pearl Harbor" was unrivaled as the American synonym for "surprise attack." President Franklin D. Roosevelt called December 7, 1941, a day "which will live in infamy." For Nikkei, it was the beginning of a period of extreme fear and anxiety. Within twenty-four hours of the Pearl Harbor attack, FBI agents began arresting "suspicious enemy aliens," using lists that had been compiled earlier. Most of those arrested were elderly Issei community leaders who technically were aliens from an enemy nation. Headlines in Pacific Coast newspapers and statements decrying all "Japs" by public officials, such as Secretary of the Navy Frank Knox, also promoted the growing climate of anti-Japanese hysteria.

The general public believed, erroneously, that there were Japanese saboteurs active along the Pacific Coast. Newspaper columnist Henry McLemore, radio commentator John B. Hughes, California Governor Culbert Olson, California Attorney General Earl Warren, and Los Angeles Mayor Fletcher Bowron, along with a number of anti-Japanese organizations such as the American Legion and the Western Growers Protective Association, began to demand the removal of all Nikkei from the coastal areas.

A U.S. Army officer with little combat experience, Lt. General John L. DeWitt, played a major role in developing official policy toward Nikkei after December 7. DeWitt headed the Western Defense Command, which included the Pacific Coast states. On December 19, he proposed that Japanese aliens over fourteen years of age be removed from coastal areas. Other key figures in the call for incarceration of Japanese aliens included the provost marshal general of the army, General Allen W. Gullion, who wanted the Justice Department's enemy alien program transferred to the War Department—where he could control it—and Major Karl

R. Bendetsen, chief of the Aliens Division in Gullion's office. DeWitt feared sabotage by Nikkei. On January 24, 1942, he told Bendetsen: "The fact that we have had [not even] sporadic attempts at sabotage clearly means that control is being exercised somewhere else." The Roberts Commission Report on Pearl Harbor was released to the press on the next day. It erroneously reported that alleged Japanese spies "were persons having no open relations with the Japanese foreign service." Widely publicized, the Roberts Report marked the beginning of an effort to make all Nikkei appear to be a threat to national security. On January 29, U.S. Attorney General Francis Biddle announced that enemy aliens would be removed from designated strategic areas along the Pacific Coast.

On February 1, a meeting was held in Washington, D.C. In attendance were Biddle, Gullion, Bendetsen, FBI Director J. Edgar Hoover, and Assistant Secretary of War John McCloy. When Biddle adamantly refused to evict U.S. citizens from their rightful homes, McCloy declared: ". . . if it is [a] question of the safety of the country [and] the Constitution . . . the Constitution is just a scrap of paper." DeWitt declared that "all . . . Japs of American citizenship" should be removed. On February 4, Governor Olson announced that "it is known that there are Japanese residents of California who have sought to aid the Japanese enemy by way of communicating information, or have shown indications of preparation for fifth column activities." Olson added that he and General DeWitt had agreed upon plans for the "movement and placement of the entire adult Japanese population in California . . . under such surveillance and protection . . . as shall be deemed necessary." Los Angeles Mayor Bowron pointed out that "right here in our own city are those who may spring to action at an appointed time in accordance with a prearranged plan wherein each of our little Japanese friends will know his part in the event of any possible attempted invasion or air raid." Pacific Coast congressmen, led by Senator Hiram Johnson of California, began to coordinate their anti-Japanese activities, and the press began to clamor for the mass removal of all Nikkei to places deeper in the nation's interior.

The civil rights of Nikkei was not a popular cause at the time. Few Americans opposed the mass removal. Unlike the uneven performance of some of his colleagues in the American Civil Liberties Union (ACLU), attorney A. L. Wirin argued that "treating persons, because they are members of a race, constitutes illegal discrimination, which is forbidden by the Fourteenth Amendment whether we are at war or peace." A few religious leaders and groups, such as the Quakers, provided some humanitarian support during the Nikkei wartime diaspora, but their activities had no influence on those who advised the president.

Executive Order 9066: "Military Necessity"?

On February 6, Gullion wrote to McCloy that "from reliable reports from military and other sources, the danger of Japanese-inspired sabotage is great . . . . No half-way measures based upon considerations of economic disturbance, humanitarianism, or fear of retaliation will suffice." Gullion and Bendetsen recommended that all alien Japanese and their families be confined east of the Sierra Nevada Mountains. On February 11, McCloy and Secretary of War Henry Stimson asked President Roosevelt if he would authorize the mass removal of Japanese aliens and citizens from restricted areas. McCloy reported that the president had cautioned, "be as reasonable as you can," but encouraged them to "go ahead and do anything you think necessary . . . ." On February 13, a Pacific Coast congressional delegation recommended to the president "the immediate evacuation of all persons of Japanese lineage . . . aliens and citizens alike, whose presence shall be deemed dangerous or inimical to the defense of the United States . . . ." The next day, DeWitt sent a memo to Stimson, recommending mass removal of "Japanese and other subversive persons" from the Pacific Coast.

On Thursday, February 19, 1942, President Roosevelt signed Executive Order 9066. It authorized and directed "the Secretary of War and the Military Commanders whom he may . . . designate to prescribe . . . military areas . . . from which any or all persons may be excluded. . . ." Secretary Stimson placed DeWitt in charge of the program.

Two days later, a committee headed by California representative John H. Tolan convened in San Francisco to investigate "National Defense Migration." The testimonies of witnesses overwhelmingly supported the need to remove all Nikkei. One witness was California Attorney General Earl Warren, a gubernatorial candidate, who warned of Japanese spies and sabotage: "I believe that we are just being lulled into a false sense of security and the only reason we haven't had a disaster in California is because it has been timed for a different date. . . . Our day of reckoning is bound to come in that regard . . .," and "every citizen must give up some of his rights" in wartime. When asked whether or not the mass removal was constitutional, Warren replied that it was "absolutely constitutional."

Roosevelt's issuance of Executive Order 9066 was based on the false claim of "military necessity." There is no question that, by February 19, 1942, the news was grim. Manila and most of the Philippines, Hong Kong, and Singapore had fallen to Japan, and the Dutch East Indies and Burma were under siege. But if the Nikkei on the West Coast were a threat to national security, why weren't Hawaiian Nikkei removed from their homes and locked up? The 157,000 Nikkei in Hawaii constituted more than one-third of the Islands' total population, and Hawaii anchored U.S. defenses in the Pacific. Navy Secretary Frank Knox's plan had Roosevelt's full support: all Nikkei on Oahu would be placed on the island of Molokai, the home of the leper colony. But the mass removal of Hawaiian Nikkei to Molokai or to mainland concentration camps never occurred because Nikkei workers could not be economically replaced and no ships were available to transport them. As a result, less than 1 percent of Hawaii's total Nikkei population was incarcerated at sites, such as Sand Island Detention Camp in Honolulu Harbor; and from those less than 2,000 Hawaiian Nikkei were transported to the mainland concentration camps.

On the Pacific Coast, Nikkei were faced with the dilemma of accepting the mass expulsion order or challenging the awesome resources of an explicitly racist and paranoid government. With the arrest and removal of virtually all Issei community leaders within hours after Pearl Harbor, the role of Nikkei community spokespersons was filled by Nisei "200 percenters," such as those who had founded the Japanese American Citizens League (JACL) in 1930. In 1941 the JACL was a small organization. For example, out of the 24,000 Nisei in Los Angeles County, it could claim barely 600 members. During the war years the JACL claimed a national membership of 30,000 (of whom a mere 1,800 paid dues). Attracting acculturated, ambitious, young adult Nisei who rejected the language and culture of their ancestors as impediments to acceptance into the mainstream U.S. society, the JACL embraced accommodation over confrontation as a survival strategy in the explicitly racist and nativist environment of the times. JACL National Secretary Mike Masaoka seized the opportunity to ingratiate the organization with the federal government and urged all Nikkei to cooperate with Executive Order 9066 without question. Those who demanded their rights as citizens, such as James Omura, the JACL ostracized. JACL members actively collaborated with civilian and military officials throughout the war in identifying other Nikkei as "troublemakers" and potential "disloyals." Apologists for JACL claim, in retrospect, that amidst the war hysteria caused by the "sneak attack" on Pearl Harbor, there was very little that their members or any Nikkei could have done beyond declaring their own loyalty to the United States. Nevertheless, the organization's wartime advocacy of total "cooperation" without demanding due process or other constitutional guarantees remains a source of bitterness among Nikkei.

Mass Removal of "All Persons of Japanese Ancestry"

On March 11, one day before the Tolan Committee's hearings on National Defense Migration were concluded, General DeWitt created the Wartime Civil Control Administration (WCCA) to handle the expulsion of Nikkei from the Pacific Coast and appointed (the newly promoted) Colonel Bendetsen as the administration's director. Beginning with the March 30 removal of Nikkei on Bainbridge Island, Washington, the WCCA posted in public places "Civilian

Exclusion Orders" with "Instructions to All Persons of Japanese Ancestry Living in the Following Area. . . ." Each single person and head of family was to register at a WCCA control station, where they would receive a family number and identification tags. At this point they were usually given a week to dispose of all their belongings and report to a local neighborhood site where, guarded by armed military police and in full view of onlookers, they boarded the busses or trains to larger assembly centers. The "shame and humiliation," said one Nisei, was "something I will remember about the good ol' U.S.A. until the day I die."

More than 21,000 persons were sent directly to "permanent" camps like the Colorado River WRA concentration camp (Poston) in the Arizona desert, and Manzanar, at the barren base of Mt. Whitney in California—where incarcerees were forced to help build their own barracks. The majority were housed in makeshift "assembly centers," where hastily-strung barbed wire enclosed such places as county fairgrounds, racetracks, and livestock exposition facilities. Once in the assembly centers, Nikkei families had to sleep in horse stalls or crudely constructed tarpaper shelters, eat in crowded mess halls, and bathe in communal showers. Toilet stalls were forbidden, and one incarceree recalled, "there was no privacy of any kind. My mom, my sisters and my grandma were mortified to be naked in the presence of strangers." It was only after heated and sustained protests by religious groups that crude partitions, but still without doors, were eventually erected in women's latrines in some camps.

The number of Nikkei incarcerees and the period of existence of each assembly center varied from 245 persons at Mayer, Arizona (May 7 to June 21), to 18,719 persons at Santa Anita Racetrack in Los Angeles (May 7 to October 27). By early August 1942, the U.S. Army announced that 110,723 persons had been removed from their homes along the Pacific Coast and placed in temporary assembly centers while ten permanent "relocation centers" were being constructed.

The mass removal could have stopped there, before Nikkei were moved farther from their homes. By the end of June 1942, U.S. intelligence agencies knew that the Battle of Midway had eliminated the threat of a Japanese invasion of Hawaii or the Pacific Coast. Nonetheless, lucrative construction contracts were signed and many jobs were created as the construction of primitive tarpaper barracks continued in remote regions of the nation. The Army insisted that the camps be located "at a safe distance" from industrial centers and other strategic sites. Thus, the Nikkei became political prisoners in a vast gulag of concentration camps hundreds and in many cases thousands of miles away from their homes.

A still little-known dimension to the mass removal was an ominous plan to use Nikkei as human barter, in exchange for U.S. prisoners of war held by Imperial Japan. This led to the arrest and deportation of more than 2,300 Japanese residents, most of them citizens of several Latin American nations, to the United States in 1942–43. The scheme did not involve the 23,000 Canadian Japanese who were removed from British Columbia and incarcerated in that nation's own system of concentration camps (under the benign official euphemism "Interior Housing Projects"). The U.S. State Department solicited and transported deportees from more than a dozen Latin American nations, at U.S. expense, to U.S. Justice Department camps, such as

Crystal City, Texas. The Latin American deportees were later scattered among the camps for Nikkei; of these the majority came from Peru, where Japanese immigrants were strongly resented. Cooperating nations were wooed by several incentives, including expeditious delivery of promised Lend-Lease military equipment.

ADMINISTERING THE CONCENTRATION CAMPS

A month after he issued Executive Order 9066, President Roosevelt established the civilian-staffed War Relocation Authority (WRA). After serving as the first director for only three months, Milton Eisenhower was replaced by Dillon S. Myer. Myer and WRA apologists worked hard to create the impression that America's concentration camps for Nikkei, while an unfortunate "necessity," were models of humane and benevolent administration. The JACL, whose wartime policy had been obsequious cooperation with WRA officials, honored Myer as a "champion of human rights." But the realities of the physical and psychological environment created by Myer and WRA camp administrators, as seen from the inmates' perspective, suggest a much less idyllic experience than that portrayed by the apologists.

The WRA existed for one purpose: to build and operate a vast gulag of ten major concentration camps and supporting facilities, officially known as "Relocation Centers," for the imprisonment of 110,000 men, women, and children, the majority of whom were U.S. citizens. The camps were enclosed by barbed-wire fences and guard towers equipped with machine guns and searchlights; inside, military police had orders to shoot anyone attempting to escape. To monitor and manipulate the large and potentially volatile number of understandably frustrated and angry inmates, an intricate network of collaborators and informants was established, among whom JACL members were active. To deter and punish dissident activity, the WRA directly and indirectly employed the threat of isolation, exile, forced labor, public humiliation, and even torture and death.

With the exception of Tule Lake in northern California and Manzanar on the eastern side of the Sierra Nevada range, all of the eight other "permanent" WRA Relocation Centers were located in states a long distance away from the Pacific Coast: Colorado River, at Poston, and Gila River in Arizona; Rohwer and Jerome in Arkansas; Minidoka in Idaho; Heart Mountain, in Wyoming; Granada, at Amache, in Colorado; and Central Utah, at Topaz, in Utah. Without exception, the sites chosen for the camps were harshly inhospitable: eight were located in unirrigated deserts known to experience debilitating dust storms, harsh summers, and freezing winters; the Arkansas sites were located in heavily wooded and undrained swampland.

Still largely unknown was the existence of a large and intricate network of special "isolation centers." Established at remote and easily isolated sites, such as Moab, Utah, and Leupp, Arizona, the secretive and sinister image of these facilities gave them a notoriety that WRA was quick to exploit in its efforts to deter incarcerees from "troublemaking" (any activity defined by the WRA as dissent or protest). Issei were threatened with exile to alien internment camps operated by the Immigration and Naturalization Service (INS) at places such as Crystal City and Seagoville, Texas, and Santa Fe, New Mexico, under auspices of the Department of Justice. Federal government suppression of information and bureaucratic officiousness still obscure and obstruct research on the exact location of and the specific activities conducted at each site.

LIFE BEHIND BARBED WIRE

Inside the "Relocation Centers," WRA administrators and staff were housed in spacious and well-furnished residential facilities constructed by the inmates. All other living quarters in the camps were crude and austere black tarpaper barracks built to the specifications used to house single male Army recruits. Five families were assigned to each barrack, with a standard GI-issue single cot for each person. As in the temporary assembly centers, eating, bathing, and toilet facilities were all communal, and the lack of personal privacy served as a constant reminder to the residents of the camps that they were indeed prisoners. One former inmate recalled:

> *We lined up together for everything—cheek to cheek, tit to tit, and butt to butt. In order to build partitions to separate families, or kids from married couples, we first hung blankets or pieces of cloth. But it was so cold, we needed the blankets. Later, us kids slipped into the restricted lumber area and stole wood. But even then everyone could hear everything—from whispered lovemaking, to farts and family arguments . . . day after day, week after week . . . .*

Nisei who were teenagers at the time remember that they "had a great time . . . staying out late . . . hanging out with friends . . . ." Their comments are not surprising, for within the communal environment, traditional family roles often eroded and disintegrated. Many husbands took their meals with male friends in distant mess halls and rarely ate with their own families.

Petty differences and mundane needs became inflated imbroglios. The use of a vacant meeting room could be fought over with equal passion by Christians and Buddhists or poker players, pimps, and panderers seeking to expand their services. There were few secrets, for the "grapevine" caught everything, from "who had hemorrhoids to who was cheating on his wife." Rumors were rife about *inu* ("dog")— collaborators—who informed on those who complained about the "lousy food" or the denial of their constitutional rights as U.S. citizens. There was also fear of the kind that only those who have experienced incarceration can appreciate—fear that the Military Police (MP) truck would pull up outside your barrack in the middle of the night and take you or a loved one away to the special WRA isolation camps, first at Moab, Utah, and later at Leupp, Arizona. When those sites were closed, "dissidents" were concentrated at Tule Lake, California. These episodes explain the lingering resentments harbored by some Nisei toward other inmates in the same camp.

Inmates with professional skills found jobs in the camps, but whereas white civilians employed by the WRA received standard wages, Nisei doctors and teachers received inmate pay of $19 a month. The least skilled jobs paid $12 a month. WRA work policy restricted temporary off-camp employment to stoop-labor agricultural tasks, which posed no competition to private industry; thus some 10,000 incarcerees worked as seasonal farm workers, picking crops like sugar beets. These migratory labor teams ranged from the Mississippi Delta to the slopes of the Rocky Mountains and worked under varied conditions—from close scrutiny by armed guards to near autonomy. While outside the camps, the workers were forced to carry identification cards that stated the location and duration of their authorized assignments.

Incarcerees were aware that the WRA employed social scientists to observe inmate behavior and advise camp administrators on how to maintain control. But most Nikkei were unaware of a covert social science research project started at the Berkeley campus of the University of California, the Japanese American Evacuation and Resettlement Study (JERS), during the spring of 1942—amid the initial mass uprooting of Nikkei on the West Coast. Directed by sociologist Dorothy Swaine Thomas, who had no prior interest in or experience with Nikkei or Japanese studies, JERS employed Thomas' graduate students, including Nikkei incarcerees, to serve as "participant observers" who secretly recorded copious notes on daily life in the WRA concentration camps. Ostensibly independent of the WRA, the JERS generated project files that constitute a meticulously detailed and comprehensive record of the wartime Nikkei gulag and diaspora, one yet to be systematically mined by researchers for evidence of contacts, if not cooperation between, the two organizations. Two of the first scholarly books on the incarceration were JERS products published by the University of California Press: *The Spoilage* (1946) by Dorothy S. Thomas and Richard S. Nishimoto, on allegedly disloyal Nikkei at Tule Lake; and Thomas' *The Salvage* (1952) on Nikkei who left the camps during the war for jobs or schooling.

Some college students were eventually aided by educators, such as Robert Gordon Sproul, president of the University of California. He and organizations like the Quakers and the National Japanese Student Relocation Council contacted campuses throughout the country in an effort to get qualified Nisei out of the camps and back to their studies. Strong opposition faced the college program from such groups as the American Legion and the University of Southern California, where President Rufus B. von Kleinsmid refused to transmit transcripts on the grounds that to do so would be to aid and abet the enemy. Princeton, the Massachusetts Institute of Technology, and Indiana University were among many other campuses that declined to accept Nikkei. Only 4,300 students left the camps, and the federal government refused to provide financial assistance, aside from WRA funds allotted for travel expenses. Private citizens and religious groups deserve credit for finding jobs and housing, and defraying tuition fees for the fortunate Nikkei students who escaped the gulag.

Violence and Death by Deadly Force

Daily life behind barbed wire was not without resistance or violence. A variety of acts of mischief and defiance of authority served as safety valves for smoldering frustrations, but there were several instances when tensions flared into large and violent confrontations. MPs assigned to each camp were on duty as "guards," not "sentries"; their mission was to keep the inmates in, not to repel outsiders. While America's concentration camps for Nikkei cannot be equated with Nazi death camps, it should not be overlooked that Nikkei inmates were beaten, shot, and killed—some by camp guards, some by each other. One of the earliest examples of violence came on August 4, 1942, at the assembly center at Santa Anita racetrack. A crowd of Nikkei harassed civilian police who had confiscated hotplates, Japanese reading materials, and phonograph records. The protesters also assaulted a Nikkei whom they suspected of being an informant for the police.

In November 1942, a general strike was called at the Colorado River WRA camp at Poston after it was learned that two Kibei accused of beating another Kibei would be tried outside the camp. One thousand inmates gathered to demand the prisoners' release, the elected community council resigned, pickets marched, inmates refused to perform all manner of assigned jobs, and the camp became dysfunctional. After ten days, the camp's administration capitulated. One Kibei was freed and the other was tried in the camp.

On December 6, 1942, a mass demonstration broke out at Manzanar when several Kibei were arrested for assaulting Fred Tayama, a Nisei JACL member whom they suspected of being an informant for the camp administration. The angry mob pushed into the hospital in an effort to kill the recuperating victim, while others stormed the jail in hopes of freeing Harry Ueno, a Kibei who had attempted to organize kitchen workers and accused WRA officials of depriving incarcerees of food by misusing mess hall funds. When the crowd at the jail failed to disperse, shots were fired. Before the whole incident had ended, two men were dead and ten more were wounded. Nearly a month passed before some semblance of normal conditions was restored at the camp.

On April 11, 1943, a sixty-three-year-old Issei bachelor named James Hatsuki Wakasa was shot and killed by a sentry in a guard tower at WRA Camp Topaz, Utah. The uproar over Wakasa's killing forced an investigation that revealed that the U.S. Army had lied when it reported that the old man had been shot while trying to escape by crawling through the camp's barbed-wire fence. Moreover, the army engaged in a cover-up in an attempt to hide the lie. Finally, the incident was exploited as an excuse to harass the inmates at Topaz, and MPs were issued Thompson submachine guns and gas masks.

Nikkei inmates who were shot and killed by guards include Shoichi James Okamoto on May 24,1944, at Tule Lake. After July 15, 1943, Tule Lake concentration camp was designated as the sole WRA Segregation Center for incarcerees assumed to be "disloyal" or "troublemakers" due to allegations by Nikkei informants (*inu*) or because they either refused to answer or said "no-no" to questions 27 and 28 on the loyalty questionnaire (see p. 29). By the spring of 1944, Tule Lake was the largest WRA concentration camp, imprisoning over 18,000 Nikkei men, women, and children in facilities constructed to house 15,000 persons. Many inmates at Tule Lake suffered at least two or more dislocations as they were shipped from other confinement sites in the WRA gulag. Spouses and families were separated, as individuals were sent to and from prisons administered by the Department of Justice and INS.

Harassed by fellow Nikkei who served as WRA informants, intimidated by threats from WRA staff, and confused by misinformation and disinformation from competing Nisei and Kibei factions, those incarcerated at Tule Lake described the atmosphere within as akin to an asylum. Overcrowding, poor food and accommodations, inadequate medical care, labor disputes, black-market profiteering, and racist staff all led to organized demonstrations against the WRA administration, who in turn treated incarcerees as prisoners without rights, refused to negotiate with moderates, and retaliated with punitive measures. Martial law was imposed at Tule Lake from November 1943 to January 1944. Military control was enforced by a battalion of 1,000 U.S. Army military police in battle gear, who created and maintained an atmosphere of fear through midnight surprise sweeps, with fixed bayonets, in search of so-called troublemakers. The troops were supported by tanks, an eight-foot-high, double "man-proofed" barbed-wire fence, and the notorious "stockade," where troublemakers were imprisoned and isolated for weeks and months without charges or due process. An FBI report on August 2, 1945, noted that three Nikkei incarcerees were "suspected of dissident behavior . . . detained, savagely beaten, tortured and thrown into the stockade. One . . . suffered permanent mental impairment, one committed suicide, and the third, disillusioned with American justice, renounced [his U. S. citizenship] and expatriated to Japan."

The Botched Loyalty Questionnaire

The idea of segregating "loyal" Japanese Americans from those who could not "prove" their loyalty originated as early as 1942. Rejected at first, the idea took root in January 1943 when the army informed WRA director Dillon Myer of its decision to form an all-Nisei volunteer combat unit composed of Japanese Americans from the camps and from Hawaii. In order to ensure that only "loyal" young men were inducted into the unit, the army suggested that a questionnaire be administered to males of draft age. The Selective Service Form 304A, "Statement of United States Citizen of Japanese Ancestry," contained a total of twenty-eight questions, including:

> 27. *Are you willing to serve in the armed forces of the United States on combat duty, wherever ordered?*

28. Will you swear unqualified allegiance to the United States of America and faithfully defend the United States from any or all attack by foreign or domestic forces, and forswear any form of allegiance or obedience to the Japanese emperor, or any other foreign government, power, or organization?

In February, the WRA decided to distribute hastily edited versions of the army's questionnaire to *all* incarcerees. The questionnaire was vague and clumsily worded. Its very title, "Application for Leave Clearance," confused Issei who had no desire to leave the country. The real problems, however, were caused by questions 27 and 28:

27. If the opportunity presents itself and you are found qualified, would you be willing to volunteer for the Army Nurse Corps or the WAAC [Women's Army Auxiliary Corps]?
28. Will you swear unqualified allegiance to the United States of America and forswear any form of allegiance or obedience to the Japanese emperor, or any other foreign government, power or organization?

Many cautious Issei and Nisei women refused to volunteer for combat duty as Question 27 requested—after all, they had learned that the government could not be trusted. Question 28 violated the Geneva Convention regarding the treatment of enemy aliens when Issei, who were denied U.S. citizenship, were asked to voluntarily become stateless—neither American nor Japanese. Although Question 28 was rewritten for Issei to read "will you swear to abide by the laws of the United States and to take no actions which would in any way interfere in the war effort of the United States," the damage had already been done. Even Nisei were perplexed by the questions. For example, would a "yes" response to Question 28 mean that an allegiance to Japan existed? Of those eligible to register (78,000 inmates), 7,600 or 11 percent gave "no" or qualified answers to the loyalty question.

When the WRA reviewed the loyalty questionnaire, those inmates deemed as "disloyal" were shipped to Tule Lake concentration camp, where they ultimately comprised about two-thirds of the 18,000 inmates there. It was from among the angry and alienated incarcerees at Tule Lake that the Justice Department received letters expressing a desire to repatriate to Japan. In July 1944 Congress passed a law that permitted those who wished to renounce their citizenship to do so. While this was in part a direct response to the Tuleans, it was also an attempt to appease the many nativist groups who had long wanted to get rid of all Nikkei permanently.

After the exclusion order was lifted in January 1945, a mass "renunciation fever" swept Tule Lake, leading thousands to cast away their U.S. citizenship. Months later, realizing the rashness of that decision, many renunciants asked to have their applications for renouncements withdrawn, claiming that they had acted out of duress. The Justice Department claimed that the attorney general did not have the power to restore citizenship lost in this manner. The legal battle over the issue, spearheaded by San Francisco attorney Wayne Collins on behalf of those who wished to regain their U.S. citizenship, lasted for decades. By the end of May 1959, citizenship was restored to 4,978 renunciants and to 1,327 of the original 2,031 renunciants who had left for Japan.

Collins fought on until 1968, succeeding in the restoration of citizenship to nearly all those who sought it.

Nikkei Soldiers and Draft Resisters

The original intent of the loyalty questionnaire had been to attract 3,500 volunteers for an all-Nikkei combat unit. By now the government was finally worried that the existence of concentration camps housing American citizens was bound to create embarrassing questions for the "land of the free" at the end of the war, and a claim that Nikkei had patriotically volunteered to fight (and die) for the United States would provide both the JACL and the government with positive publicity. President Roosevelt enthusiastically endorsed the program. The response from Nisei in Hawaii was encouraging, with 10,000 volunteers stepping forth. But in the real target area of recruitment, the mainland camps, a mere 1,200 of the estimated 10,000 eligible Nikkei answered the call. As Army officials scurried about in search of ways to avoid a public relations fiasco, a stop-gap measure was found in the 100th Battalion, a Hawaiian National Guard unit composed of Nisei.

Hawaiian Nisei of the 100th Battalion arrived for training at Camp Shelby, Mississippi, in April 1943—the same day that General DeWitt told the House Naval Affairs Subcommittee in San Francisco that "a Jap's a Jap . . . ." By autumn of 1943 the 100th Battalion had seen heavy fighting in Italy. Their exemplary combat record and their high marks while in training convinced the War Department to proceed with plans for the formation of a larger unit.

There remained, however, the problem of attracting sufficient numbers of Nisei volunteers from the mainland concentration camps, for the inmates had not forgotten the clumsily handled loyalty questionnaire. The army resorted to the one sure method of creating a large, all-Nisei combat unit on January 24, 1944, when Secretary of War Stimson declared that Selective Service rights (meaning the right to be drafted) would be restored to all Nikkei because of the excellent performance of those Nisei already in service. He failed to mention that conscription was necessary because of the lack of volunteers. A month later, on February 24, 1944, the military revealed its dire manpower needs by announcing that even Japanese aliens would be allowed to volunteer for military service.

More than 25,778 Nikkei, including several hundred women, served in World War II. While hundreds were assigned as translators and Military Intelligence Service operatives in the Pacific theater and in Asia, the best-known Nikkei units were the racially segregated 100th Battalion and the 442nd Regimental Combat Team, whose motto was "Go For Broke" (Hawaiian crapshooters' slang for "shoot the works").

By the early summer of 1944, the first elements of the 442nd Regimental Combat Team, consisting of three battalions (one of which was the 100th from Hawaii) landed in Italy. Army and WRA public-relations experts later publicized them as "the most heavily decorated unit in the history of the U.S. Army." The 442nd's statistics were indeed impressive: in seven major European campaigns the 442nd suffered 9,486 casualties (or 300 percent of the unit's original strength), and earned 18,000 individual medals (including one Medal of Honor and 52 Distinguished Service Crosses). While groups such as the JACL proclaimed the heavy losses suffered by the 442nd as a necessary, albeit costly, sacrifice for the goal of returning full civil liberties to Japanese Americans, there were those within the camps who did not agree. One Nisei who refused his draft call remarked bitterly:

> Baka *["stupid"]! Why should we get killed! How can you tell me that we're fighting dirty Nazis to defend 'democracy' and the 'Four Freedoms' when our wives, kids, and families are left behind . . . rotting in America's own stinking concentration camps? Let us out . . . and then maybe I'll think about risking my skin for 'the land of the free.'*

The award of only one Medal of Honor to a Nikkei soldier, given posthumously to Army Pfc. Sadao S. Munemori, who died in action with the 442nd in Italy on April 5, 1945, raised questions for years. The issue was finally resolved a half-century later, after an investigation concluded that racism had indeed played a role in denying medals to soldiers of color. On June 21, 2000, President Bill Clinton awarded Medals of Honor to twenty Nisei veterans of World War II, including Senator Daniel Inouye, who lost an arm in combat in Italy.

A small but steadfast minority, eventually totaling more than 200 young men, did oppose the draft. At the WRA prison camp at Heart Mountain, Wyoming, resisters organized as the Fair Play Committee challenged the constitutionality of their mass imprisonment and demanded their freedom as a condition of accepting conscription. The JACL-dominated camp newspaper, the *Heart Mountain Sentinel*, supported the draft, but James Omura's editorials in the Denver *Rocky Shimpo* criticized the JACL's campaign for military service as a desertion of "justice, fair play, equal rights and all that are revered in our constitution and in the government of the United States." JACL collaborators and WRA officials brutally suppressed the Nikkei draft-resistance movement. Resisters were separated from their families and exiled to other camps. At Heart Mountain alone, eighty-five resisters were convicted, and the Supreme Court refused to review their cases. The director of the American Civil Liberties Union, Roger Baldwin, publicly refused any support for Fair Play Committee members. As a result, most inmates complied with the draft and reported dutifully to the nearest induction center.

THE WARTIME SUPREME COURT TEST CASES

In 1942, four young Pacific Coast Nisei, who had never met one another, separately challenged the government's policies and pressed their cases all the way to the U.S. Supreme Court. The court's majority rulings in these "Japanese American cases" sanctioned the denial of basic civil rights of U.S. citizens by reason of their race.

The first Japanese American to challenge General De-Witt's curfew order was Minoru Yasui, born in 1916 to Issei apple growers in Hood River, Oregon, who believed in the American Dream. All seven children in Yasui's family were raised as Methodists and sent to college. After the attack on Pearl Harbor, Yasui, a graduate of the University of Oregon law school, immediately resigned from his job at the Japanese consulate in Chicago and reported for duty as a commissioned officer in the U.S. Army Reserve. When he arrived at Fort Vancouver, however, he was ordered off the base no less than eight times. Shortly thereafter, his father was arrested because he had been identified as an Issei community leader, and he was sent to the Justice Department concentration camp in Missoula, Montana, where young Yasui was denied permission to serve as his father's legal counsel. On Saturday night, March 28, 1942, in Portland, a livid Yasui demanded to be arrested for violating the military curfew, and he later served nearly a year in solitary confinement. In *Yasui* v. *United States,* a federal judge found him guilty of curfew violation on the rationale that he had forfeited his U.S. citizenship by working for the Japanese consulate and, as an "enemy alien," had to obey the curfew. Later, when Yasui's case eventually reached the U.S. Supreme Court, it was returned to Portland, where the original decision was set aside to comply with the Supreme Court's decision in the case of *Hirabayashi* v. *United States.*

On May 16, 1942, Gordon Kiyoshi Hirabayashi presented a typed statement to FBI agents in Seattle: "I must maintain my Christian principles. I consider it my duty to maintain the democratic standards for which this nation lives. Therefore, I must refuse this order for evacuation." Hirabayashi was twenty-four years old, a senior at the University of Washington, and a volunteer with a Quaker group who assisted Nikkei caught up in the mass removal. Angered by the military curfew placed solely on Nikkei, he decided to offer himself up as a test case. He was arrested and convicted for refusing to obey the army's curfew order and for failing to report for removal by the army. On June 21, 1943, in *Hirabayashi* v. *United States,* the Supreme Court unanimously upheld the racist curfew policy while refusing to deal with the constitutionality of the mass removal. Chief Justice Harlan Fiske Stone reasoned that, "in time of war residents having ethnic affiliations with an invading enemy may be a greater source of danger than those of a different ancestry."

Another case affected by the court's ruling was that of Fred Toyosaburo Korematsu, a twenty-three-year-old welder who underwent minor plastic surgery in an effort to evade the exclusion order and stay with his white girl friend. It was after he was arrested and sent to Tanforan assembly center to await trial that Korematsu decided to become a test-case plaintiff. The Supreme Court's decision in *Hirabayashi* had focused narrowly on the army's curfew imposed in the early months of the war. The broader issue of the entire program of mass curfew, exclusion, and incarceration was up for review when the court issued its ruling in *Korematsu* v. *United States,* on December 18, 1944. With three justices dissenting, the majority upheld Korematsu's conviction solely on the government's claim of "military necessity." In Justice Hugo Black's majority opinion: "Korematsu was not excluded from the military area because of hostility to him or his race. He was excluded because we are at war with the Japanese Empire, because the properly constituted military authorities feared an invasion of our West Coast . . . ."

In his scathing dissent "from this legalization of racism . . . ," Justice Frank Murphy excoriated DeWitt for perpetuating racist stereotypes and challenged the validity of the government's reliance on "military necessity" as its rationale for the entire incarceration program: "This forced exclusion was the result in good measure of this erroneous assumption of racial guilt rather than bona fide military necessity . . . [DeWitt] refers to all individuals of Japanese descent as 'subversive,' as belonging to 'an enemy race' whose 'racial strains are undiluted' . . . ."

The highest court in the land released its ruling on the fourth case, *Ex parte Endo,* on the same day as *Korematsu*. Instead of challenging the curfew and exclusion orders directly, Mitsuye Endo waited until she was incarcerated at central Utah (Topaz) and then applied for a writ of *ha-*

beas corpus. The twenty-two-year-old Methodist had been a clerical worker in the California Department of Motor Vehicles in Sacramento. She could not speak or write Japanese, had never visited Japan, and had a brother in the U.S. Army. Endo rejected a WRA offer of immediate freedom if she would agree to abandon her legal challenge, and she remained incarcerated for more than two years until the court finally ordered her released. The unanimous decision, according to Justice William O. Douglas, was that Endo had been detained not by the military but "by a civilian agency, the [WRA] . . . which [had] no authority to [detain] citizens who are concededly loyal . . . ." Justice Murphy added that "detention in Relocation Centers of persons of Japanese ancestry regardless of loyalty is . . . another example of the unconstitutional resort to racism inherent in the entire evacuation program."

After *Endo* and *Korematsu,* Yale University law professor Eugene Rostow immediately attacked the Supreme Court's "bewildering and unimpressive series of opinions" in the Japanese American cases. Rostow supported Justice Murphy's dissenting position that the government's claim of "military necessity" was based on DeWitt's racism rather than on factual evidence, and he urged that "the basic issues should be presented to the Supreme Court again, in an effort to obtain a reversal of these war-time cases."

RELEASE AND RETURN

During the last half of the incarceration—because of the departure of young adults—to do farm work, attend college, or serve in the armed forces—the camps were mostly populated by the very young and the very old. As early as

1943, the WRA began to encourage "voluntary" departures from the camps, and thus began the first step on "the road back." Many Issei could not cope with the trauma of another uprooting, of returning to the racial hostility of the West Coast, of rebuilding all that had been so ruthlessly taken from them. Old, frightened, and ashamed, some committed suicide. By the time the original orders for mass removal and incarceration were rescinded on January 2, 1945, nearly 20 percent of the Issei remained in the camps, and half of the original inmate population remained in them. When the camps finally closed, the remaining inmates had to be forced outside the gates.

The Nikkei recovery from their wartime diaspora was accomplished with minimal financial assistance from the federal government, though attempts were made on the Pacific Coast to facilitate their return. One such effort was the Pacific Coast Committee on American Principles and Fair Play. Acting as an umbrella for private, federal, state, and local groups and agencies, as well as African American, Filipino, and Korean community organizations, the committee agreed that "any attempt to make capital for their racial groups at the expense of the Japanese would be sawing off the limbs on which they themselves sat." Such gratuitous rhetoric, however, did little to aid returnees facing the enormous challenge of reuniting families, finding shelter, reestablishing businesses, and earning a living.

Nikkei returned to find that household possessions stored in warehouses had been stolen, while businesses and farms had been stripped of equipment. Many properties and businesses were legally lost because white "friends" refused to sell them back to the returnees, and Nikkei farmers who had leased their land found their fields lying fallow. In California, the government sought to deny land ownership to Nikkei when the state attorney general's office aggressively initiated some eighty escheat actions against Nikkei families between 1944 and 1948. The first twenty escheat actions were initiated in 1942 by Attorney General Earl Warren, when the state appropriated $200,000 to enforce the 1920 Alien Land Law. In his successful gubernatorial campaign later that year, Warren pointedly reminded voters of his vigorous escheat actions against Japanese landowners. More than $250,000 worth of land and money were taken from Nikkei until the escheat actions finally stopped in 1952, when the California Supreme Court, in the case of *Fujii* v. *State*, declared the state's 1913 Alien Land Acts, upon which the escheat cases were based, null and void.

In 1948, when President Harry S Truman signed the Japanese [American] Evacuation Claims Act, some returnees became more hopeful about rebuilding their businesses, but the law provided no more than token compensation. The 1948 law was restricted to losses of real property, and the mere $38 million appropriated by Congress to settle 26,568 claims totaling $148 million resulted in inadequate staffing and frustrating delays in the processing of claims. Many Nikkei never filed a claim because they could not provide the required documentation; others simply did not trust the government. Forty years after the war, the Commission on Wartime Relocation and Internment of Civilians reported to Congress that "the total losses of income and property fall between $810 million and $2 billion in 1983 dollars."

In Los Angeles and other cities, returnees discovered that poor African Americans had replaced them in the inner city. The Nikkei now were forced to find housing wherever it existed; in desperation, many families formed communal residences. Then there were the everyday stresses caused the returnees by the verbal abuse and harassment heaped upon them by their fellow Americans. Men jeered and made obscene gestures at female returnees. Racist epithets were painted on walls of shops and homes. Nikkei were turned away at many markets and real estate offices. Local bureaucrats found ways to deny and delay Nikkei applications for business licenses. Insurance companies demanded that returnees forfeit their original policies and start anew at higher rates; and employers refused to count returnees' incarceration years toward accrued retirement payments.

Finally, the returnees always faced the real threat of physical violence in the cities as well as in the suburbs and rural areas. Shots were fired from cars at returnee residences in the middle of the night. Anonymous phone callers warned Nikkei merchants that their shops would be dynamited, and in many cases the threats were carried out. For many who returned to the West Coast, the long-awaited homecoming became another chapter in the nightmare that had begun in the winter of 1941 and spring of 1942.

Not all of the former inmates chose to return to the Pacific Coast. Some of them remembered the prewar hostility and decided instead to strike out for places where few if any Japanese faces had ever been seen. Of the original 110,000 incarcerees, some 43,000 scattered to states such as Illinois (15,000), Colorado (6,000), Utah (5,000), Ohio (3,900), Idaho (3,500), Michigan (2,800), New York (2,500), New Jersey (2,200), and Minnesota (1,700). California retained the largest concentration of mainland Japanese Americans in the postwar period but, by 1960, the federal census revealed that the returnees were still widely distributed throughout the nation, including unlikely areas, such as Alabama (500), Arkansas (247), Delaware (152), Iowa (599), Kentucky (774), Louisiana (519), Maine (343), Mississippi (178), New Hampshire (207), and North Dakota (127). By the mid-1960s, many of those who had left the camps to go east were still there. But some who had ventured into the Deep South and border states had begun to trickle back to the Pacific Coast.

Recovery: "Model" or "Marginal" Minority?

Back on the West Coast the 1960s saw many Nisei completing the first phase of their journey back to socioeconomic, if not psychological, recovery. The "road back" from the camps is remembered by Nisei as a frustrating period of seeking humble work wherever it was available; nonetheless, World War II was a turning point in their public image. In the conspicuous consumption climate of postwar Pacific Coast cities, Nikkei gardeners were prized status symbols, and Nikkei women were sought as uncomplaining domestics and efficient secretaries. A 1942 Gallup poll had found Nikkei to be "treacherous, cruel, sly, warlike, and hardworking." By 1961 that image was reversed, with responses such as "hardworking, artistic, intelligent, progressive, but still sly."

The highly publicized wartime heroism of the racially segregated Nikkei 442nd Regimental Combat Team had quieted questions about loyalty. Indeed, while the JACL purports to be the collective voice for Nikkei, much of the postwar acceptance occurred because Nikkei veterans formed or joined Veterans of Foreign Wars posts and other organizations, such as the American Legion, and actively exploited the political clout that veterans have traditionally enjoyed with elected officials.

Some Nikkei began to leave the temporary housing they had taken in the inner city and move into the suburbs. Many purchased their own homes and businesses, while others held civil service jobs that had been denied them before the war. There had been no Nikkei teachers in Los Angeles before the war, but by the late 1960s Nisei and *Sansei* ("third generation") teachers had become familiar faces in elementary and secondary classrooms throughout the Pacific Coast.

By the mid-1960s, many Nisei had climbed to middle-class status and soon began to exemplify the typical obsession of the nouveau riche for conspicuous consumption, the provincial conservatism of the small homeowner, and an irrational fear of "radical movements." With their interests limited generally to big cars, Nisei Week beauty pageants, bowling and golf tournaments, fishing derbys, and "keeping up with the Tanakas," typical middle-aged Nisei were "200 percent Americans." Their integration into the mainstream was reflected in the large numbers of Nikkei elected or appointed to city councils and school boards throughout the Pacific Coast. Unlike those in Hawaii, mainland Nikkei could not count on a large ethnic bloc vote, depending instead on their appeal to moderate and conservative electorates.

As the nation became preoccupied with heightening urban unrest and a violent turn in the civil rights and anti–Vietnam War movements, Nikkei did not go unnoticed. They were now hailed as the Asian counterparts of Horatio Alger who were "outwhiting the whites." Indeed, the new image of Nisei and their Sansei children among conservative whites was that of a "model minority," one whose docile and accommodationist posture should be emulated by more aggressive and impatient ethnic and feminist groups. Many conservative Nisei, including members of the JACL, carefully avoided active roles in the postwar movement for increased civil rights and social change. Seduced by the adulation heaped upon them by whites, and anxious to protect their new-found "acceptance," they were wary of activities that might possibly link them to other nonwhite minorities or "radical" movements. This attitude on the part of many Nisei parents led to a deep rift between them and their Sansei children, many of whom were by this time in high school or college and, like other people their age, fed up with the "establishment."

Many Nisei insisted that "we have made it," but the boast had a hollow ring to it. In 1960, a California survey showed that although Nikkei males were 11 percent more likely to be college graduates than their white counterparts in the state, a white male's chances of earning more than $10,000 a year was still 57 percent greater than those of Nikkei. As Sansei grew up in an increasingly multicultural environment, they resented the "model minority" stereotype as a backhanded compliment at best. Some feared that it served to pit Nikkei against other Asian Americans and invited a backlash from African Americans and Hispanics. Complaints emerged about "glass ceiling" barriers, through which top management positions could be seen but not reached by Nikkei. Sociologist Harry H. L. Kitano described Nikkei as the "middleman minority," a group that is neither at the bottom nor likely to make it to the top. American historian Martin Ridge concluded that Nikkei and other Asian Americans are "always on tap but never on top."

BREAKING THE SILENCE:
NIKKEI CONFRONT THE NIGHTMARE

Prior to the 1960s, with the exception of a few activists, most former inmates had suppressed and avoided any mention of the mass removal and incarceration, even to their Sansei children. Psychologists have described the phenomenon as a form of denial, as in the case of rape or incest in which the victim is too ashamed and humiliated to acknowledge either the act or its perpetrator.

By the late 1960s, there were signs of a growing sense of psychological security among both Nisei and Sansei about their place in American society. Generational rifts between Nisei and Sansei began to heal as Nikkei became involved in a variety of activities that saw them come to grips with their wartime past. Pilgrimages to wartime incarceration sites, known as "Days of Remembrance," were introduced on Thanksgiving weekend 1978, when a column of 2,000 people in 200 cars drove from Seattle to the Puyallup Fairgrounds that had served as an assembly center known as Camp Harmony. Days of Remembrance programs became annual events across the nation. In California, busloads of Sansei and Nisei activists made pilgrimages to the sites of former WRA concentration camps at Manzanar and Tule Lake. Activists also led a successful movement to designate the Manzanar and Tule Lake sites as official California state landmarks. Conservative Nisei opposed the use of the term "concentration camps," but all sides encouraged more historic-site designations for facilities such as fairgrounds and racetracks that had served as "assembly centers." The paucity of texts on the incarceration caused Nikkei teachers and parents to form organizations, such as the Japanese American Curriculum Project in San Mateo, California, to review and produce teaching materials on the Nikkei experience for general classroom use.

Also during this time, several controversies forced hitherto apolitical Nikkei to become activists. In 1969, a hastily organized ad hoc coalition of community and cultural groups mounted a surprisingly assertive (and suc-

cessful) protest movement against the summary firing of
Dr. Thomas Noguchi, the flamboyant Japan-born-and-
educated Los Angeles County coroner who had become a
national celebrity in the wake of Robert Kennedy's assas-
sination. On July 11, 1969, the *Los Angeles Times* printed
a full-page "Metro" section advertisement with the head-
ing: "A PLEA FOR JUSTICE, IF THIS CAN HAPPEN TO
ONE OF US, IT CAN HAPPEN TO YOU. . . . A nationally known doctor and scientist was humiliated, disgraced
and fired from a civil service post without a hearing . . .
amid charges . . . bizarre . . . degrading and odious. . . ."
Noguchi had sought JACL support, but he was rebuffed
because his strong Japanese accent and eccentric public
image did not fit that organization's preferred stereotype
of Japanese Americans as a "model minority" that avoided
public confrontations. Noguchi was eventually reinstated,
in large measure due to the unprecedented public support
from the Japanese American community.

The publication of a long-awaited JACL-sponsored history of Nikkei by Bill Hosokawa led Nisei and Sansei activists to oppose the docile stereotype perpetuated by its title:
Nisei, The Quiet Americans (1969). In stark contrast to the
JACL-sponsored history was the emergence of a prolific
body of well-received scholarly texts and revisionist publications with provocative titles, such as Roger Daniels' *Concentration Camps U.S.A: Japanese Americans and World
War II* (1971), and Michi Nishiura Weglyn's indignant insid-
er's account, *Years of Infamy: The Untold Story of America's
Concentration Camps* (1976).

More important as a turning point in the emerging as-
sertiveness was the involvement of Nikkei in the crusade
to repeal Title II—the Emergency Detention or "concentration camp" provision of the 1950 Internal Security

Act—following the revelation that concentration camps were being held in readiness for political radicals and anti– Vietnam War demonstrators. Prior to the repeal of Title II (1971), Nikkei political activism had been limited to a vocal but peripheral handful of liberal Nisei and Sansei college students. By the late 1960s, Sansei were prominent in Asian American student organizations at virtually every public and private college on the Pacific Coast. In 1981, they launched *Amerasia Journal* as "the national interdisciplinary journal of scholarship, criticism, and literature on Asian and Pacific Americans."

While conservative Nikkei-dominated organizations like the JACL resisted an activist role, new groups, such as the Asian American Political Alliance, appealed to a broad cross section of the community. The JACL's opposition to either endorsement or involvement in the movement to repeal Title II only served to widen the gap between the Nikkei community at large and the Nisei establishment represented by the JACL. Sansei troubadours, such as Chris Iijima and Nobuko Miyamoto, wrote and sang protest songs against imperialism abroad and poverty and racism at home. Nisei activists Bill and Yuri Kochiyama in New York and Sansei Warren Furutani in Los Angeles organized grassroots social justice movements. Within the JACL, a call for activism was raised by Raymond Okamura, Robert Takasugi, Bob Suzuki, and Edison Uno, who recalled: "[Opposing the "concentration camp" provision] sparked the imagination of Japanese Americans . . . who utilized the Title II issue to enlighten and sensitize politicians, public media, educators, and the general public about the gross injustices of mass incarceration . . . ."

An unexpected sign of the wider public's acceptance of Nikkei was revealed during the 1973 U.S. Senate Watergate hearings, when President Richard Nixon's attorney publicly slurred Senator Daniel Inouye as "that little Jap." The public outcry over the incident was overwhelmingly in favor of Inouye.

THE MOVEMENT FOR REDRESS

In the early 1970s, increasing unrest among Nikkei, both within and outside the JACL, prodded the cautious, Nisei-dominated organization to adopt an active civil rights role, including the demand for a fuller government accounting of its wartime treatment of Nikkei. In 1973, when the conservative JACL national president Shig Sugiyama and executive director David Ushio refused to testify in public hearings on Asian American civil rights issues conducted by the California Advisory Committee to the U.S. Commission on Civil Rights, a grassroots movement among southern California JACL chapters demanded Sugiyama's impeachment and the removal of Ushio for "misfeasance, malfeasance and nonfeasance." The impeachment movement failed, but it and other similar insurrections eventually forced the JACL to adopt a less reactionary posture.

Nikkei activists and conservatives made concessions for the appearance of community unity. Early demands for "reparations" and "compensation" from the U.S. government were eventually replaced by the less strident term "redress." Nevertheless, most established Nikkei leaders were ambivalent or hostile toward redress for fear of a public backlash until February 19, 1976, when, as part of the bicentennial celebrations of the American Revolution, President Gerald R. Ford observed that "an honest reckoning" had to acknowledge "our national mistakes" as well as "our national achievements . . . . We all know now what we should have known then—not only was that evacuation wrong, but Japanese Americans were and are loyal Americans."

Some Nikkei were satisfied with Ford's statement praising their wartime loyalty, and they considered the redress case to be closed; others, however, demanded additional action. Ford contributed to the growing momentum of the redress movement when, on his last day in office, he issued a full and unconditional pardon for Iva I. Toguri d'Aquino, the Nisei woman known as Tokyo Rose. Caught in Japan at the outbreak of World War II, she refused to renounce her U.S. citizenship but was forced by her captors to broadcast Japanese propaganda to U.S. troops, for which she was convicted (in the United States) of treason. The pardon was a victory for Clifford I. Uyeda, who had persuaded a reluctant JACL to endorse Toguri's cause, and then successfully chaired the organization's National Committee for Iva Toguri from 1975 to 1977. When Edison Uno, an early proponent of redress, died in 1977, Uyeda assumed leadership of the redress struggle within the JACL by chairing its National Committee for Redress. At the 1978 JACL convention, the redress committee circulated a pamphlet comparing the Nikkei wartime experience to that of Jews in Nazi Germany, securing a unanimous JACL endorsement to seek both an official apology (from the federal government) and a cash payment of $25,000 (later reduced to $20,000) to each incarceree.

Any semblance of Nikkei community consensus disintegrated with the announcement of JACL's addition of monetary compensation to its demand for an official apology. Nikkei conservatives were shocked, and California's Canadian-born U.S. senator, S. I. Hayakawa, immediately dismissed any notion of monetary redress as "absurd and ridiculous." Bitter differences also divided the proponents of monetary redress, and two very different strategies emerged. The first, a frontal assault to initiate a $27.5 billion class-action lawsuit in the federal courts, was organized by a new coalition called the National Council for Japanese American Redress (NC-JAR), led by William Hohri. The NCJAR had evolved from earlier efforts by Nikkei activists to seek monetary compensation through class-action lawsuits. In Seattle, activists persuaded Representative Mike Lowry (D-Wash) to introduce a House bill calling for cash payments of $15,000, plus $15 per day to each surviving incarceree, for an estimated total of $3 billion. Both the Lowry bill and NCJAR's lawsuit were unsuccessful, but the NCJAR's threat of going through the courts, and the huge monetary award they sought, helped to shape subsequent strategies and tactics of the redress movement. Less strident and less costly alternatives suddenly became more palatable to both the government and more moderate Nikkei redress advocates.

A less confrontational and lower-profile congressional "commission" strategy emerged in discussions between the symbolically crucial Nikkei congressional delegation and the JACL National Committee for Redress. The Nikkei politicians recommended the commission approach, in part to avoid the appearance of an ethnic special interest bill and to educate their colleagues and the public. This was important for the two California Nikkei members of Congress, Norman Mineta (D-San Jose, elected in 1974), and Robert Matsui (D-Sacramento, elected in 1978), who represented districts with small numbers of Nikkei voters. Overwhelming support for redress from their congressional colleagues was secured through the combined clout of the Nikkei senators from Hawaii, Democrats Spark Matsunaga and Daniel

51

Inouye. Moreover, Matsunaga and Inouye were decorated combat veterans who had served in World War II with the 442ⁿᵈ Regimental Combat Team—which effectively neutralized an anticipated backlash from some veterans groups.

The NCJAR and other proponents of class-action lawsuits angrily dismissed the commission strategy as another JACL "sellout." Even after Congress had created the Commission on Wartime Relocation and Internment of Civilians (CWRIC) in 1980, infighting divided its Nikkei supporters. The National Coalition for Redress/Reparations (NCRR), formed in 1980 and headed by Bert Nakano, was dominated by Sansei and Nisei with roots in community-based activities. NCRR agreed with the commission strategy, but it preferred a highly publicized program of public demonstrations, angry confrontations, petition and letter-writing, and maximum media exposure.

THE COMMISSION'S REPORT AND RECOMMENDATIONS

The JACL-endorsed "commission bill," which led to Congress' creation of the CWRIC, was introduced on August 2, 1979,

> to determine whether a wrong was committed against those American citizens and permanent residents relocated and/or interned as a result of Executive Order Numbered 9066 and other associated acts of the Federal Government, and to recommend appropriate remedies.

The CWRIC was chaired by Joan Z. Bernstein, former general counsel of the Department of Housing and Urban Development. Other members were Arthur S. Flemming, congressman Daniel E. Lungren, former senator Edward W.

Brooke, former congressman Robert F. Drinan, former U.S. Supreme Court justice Arthur J. Goldberg, the Reverend Ishmael V. Gromoff (an Aleut), federal judge William M. Marutani—the only Nikkei member—and former senator Hugh B. Mitchell. Because Executive Order 9066 affected Alaska's Aleuts, the commission's mandate was expanded to include an examination of their incarceration.

When President Reagan signed the Civil Liberties Act of 1988 and President George H. W. Bush issued his official apology in 1990, they were responding to the voluminous official report and recommendations of the CWRIC, which had been created by Congress and approved by President Jimmy Carter in 1980. The commission's public hearings in major cities had a profound impact on Nikkei and the general public. Aged survivors were among the most poignant of 750 witnesses who testified before the commission, and Nikkei as a community finally ended decades of silence about their wartime experience. After reviewing formerly classified records in various federal agency files, the CWRIC unanimously concluded that

> *In sum, Executive Order 9066 was not justified by military necessity, and the decisions which followed from it—detention, ending detention and ending exclusion—were not founded upon military conditions. The broad historical causes that shaped these decisions were race prejudice, war hysteria, and a failure of political leadership. Widespread ignorance about Americans of Japanese descent contributed to a policy conceived in haste and executed in an atmosphere of fear and anger at Japan. A grave injustice was done to American citizens and resident aliens of Japanese ancestry who, without any individual review*

or any probative evidence against them were excluded, removed and detained by the United States during World War II.

The commission's unanimous findings, contained in a 467-page report entitled *Personal Justice Denied* and issued in 1982, served to educate the general public and the Congress and laid a foundation for public support of the commission's two most important recommendations for further action: a presidential apology and a one-time, nontaxable $20,000 cash payment to surviving former incarcerees or their heirs.

"Military Necessity"
and the *Coram Nobis* Cases

In 1981–82, forty years after the fact, political science professor and attorney Peter Irons and CWRIC researchers Aiko Herzig-Yoshinaga and Jack Herzig discovered documents in the National Archives showing that Justice Department attorneys and army officers had withheld and altered reports attesting to the loyalty of Nikkei and had lied to the U.S. Supreme Court about the "military necessity" of the program. The unexpected discovery that the wartime test cases (see pp. 35–38) had been tainted by "fundamental error" resulting in "manifest injustice" to the defendants, led to an obscure legal proceeding, a petition for writ of error *coram nobis,* to reopen three of the four historic cases in the courts of their origin. Three legal teams were led by Sansei civil rights attorneys: Dale Minami for Fred Korematsu in San Francisco; Rod Kawakami for Gordon Hirabayashi in Seattle; and Peggy Nagae for Minoru Yasui in Portland.

Korematsu's petition was filed and decided first. In granting Korematsu's request to vacate his conviction in October 1983, U.S. District Judge Marilyn Hall Patel ruled that the evidence presented by the government to the Supreme Court had been based on "unsubstantiated facts, distortions and representations of at least one military commander, whose views were seriously affected by racism." She concluded "that the government knowingly withheld information from the courts when they were considering the critical question of military necessity in this case." Yasui's suit had sought a finding of government misconduct, but the judge declined. Yasui then filed an appeal with the Ninth Circuit Court of Appeals, but he died in November 1986, before a ruling was made.

When the Hirabayashi hearing began in June 1985, the government was determined to take the offensive. Government lawyer Victor Stone pugnaciously argued that the program of mass removal and imprisonment was justified for reasons of "military necessity," even though none of the government's witnesses could prove that a single Nikkei had been guilty of espionage. Moreover, claimed Stone, Hirabayashi's appeal to the Supreme Court back in 1943 had not been prejudiced by the suppression of evidence. U.S. District Judge Donald Voorhees was not persuaded. In February 1986, he found the government had indeed withheld evidence, and that DeWitt's actions were based solely on racism and not on "military necessity." In September 1987, the Ninth Circuit Court of Appeals vacated Hirabayashi's curfew conviction. In this ruling, Judge Mary Schroeder concluded "that there could have been no reasonable military assessment of an emergency at the time, that the orders were based upon racial stereotypes and that the orders caused needless suffering and shame for thousands of American citizens."

When the Reagan administration elected not to pursue further appeals of these lower-court decisions, hopes disappeared for a Supreme Court re-examination of the validity of imprisoning persons solely on assumptions of racial disloyalty. Although the wartime convictions in the Japanese American cases were vacated in the lower courts, the right of citizens to due process remains officially unprotected—hostage to any government claim of "military necessity."

Epilogue

Among the most enduring and important legacies of the Nikkei redress movement was the revelation of hitherto unknown information and its incorporation into a much revised and expanded official record. The CWRIC report, *Personal Justice Delayed*, and the transcripts of the *coram nobis* cases gave rise to as many new questions as they answered. One important development spawned by the movement was the emergence of institutions and organizations dedicated to preserving and perpetuating the history of the wartime Nikkei diaspora as a lesson for all Americans. These include the exhibit, *A More Perfect Union: Japanese Americans and the U.S. Constitution* in the National Museum of American History of the Smithsonian Institution; the Japanese American National Museum in Los Angeles' Little Tokyo; the National Japanese American Historical Society in San Francisco's Nihonmachi; and the National Japanese American Memorial Foundation in Washington, D.C. The remains of former WRA concentration camps at Manzanar, Tule

Lake, and Minidoka are administered as historic sites by the National Park Service (with additional sites pending approval), and numerous local memorials have been erected in honor of Nikkei veterans.

Redress arrived too late for at least half of the 120,000 incarcerees. By the start of the movement, most of the immigrant pioneer Issei had already died, and only some 60,000 of their Nisei children were still living. Among the survivors, feelings of celebration were mixed with a sense of amazement that justice so long delayed had not been denied. Supporters of the redress movement, like Congressman Mineta, hoped that "the tragedies of the internment never occur again."

On the other hand, redress left unresolved the case of Latin American Nikkei incarcerees, and cash payments of a paltry $20,000—so long after the crime occurred—given to less than half of the victims (or their heirs) hardly constitute a meaningful deterrent to future abuses of governmental power. A constitutional final accounting remains unfinished, awaiting some future case to be placed before nine political appointees to the U.S. Supreme Court.

The question looms: In the wake of "9/11," can another group of Americans be targeted for racial profiling and mass incarceration?

This map (opposite page) was used in the Commission on Wartime Relocation and Internment of Civilians' final report, *Personal Justice Denied* (p. 26). It does not include the still largely unknown but vast nationwide gulag of "temporary detention stations" and other confinement facilities for alleged Nikkei "troublemakers," such as Camp Florence and Catalina Federal Honor Camp (Arizona), East Boston (Massachusetts), Ellis Island (New York), Fort Meade (Maryland), Fort Livingston (Louisana), Fort Richardson (Alaska), Camp Forrest (Tennessee), Angel

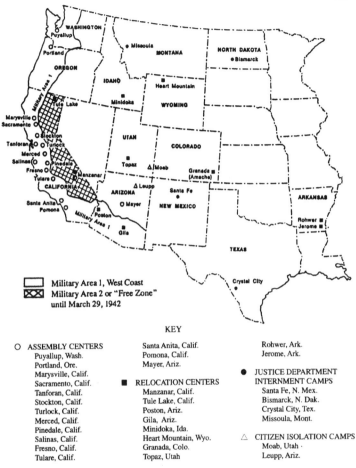

Military Area 1, West Coast
Military Area 2 or "Free Zone"
until March 29, 1942

KEY

O ASSEMBLY CENTERS
   Puyallup, Wash.
   Portland, Ore.
   Marysville, Calif.
   Sacramento, Calif.
   Tanforan, Calif.
   Stockton, Calif.
   Turlock, Calif.
   Merced, Calif.
   Pinedale, Calif.
   Salinas, Calif.
   Fresno, Calif.
   Tulare, Calif.

   Santa Anita, Calif.
   Pomona, Calif.
   Mayer, Ariz.

■ RELOCATION CENTERS
   Manzanar, Calif.
   Tule Lake, Calif.
   Poston, Ariz.
   Gila, Ariz.
   Minidoka, Ida.
   Heart Mountain, Wyo.
   Granada, Colo.
   Topaz, Utah

   Rohwer, Ark.
   Jerome, Ark.

● JUSTICE DEPARTMENT
   INTERNMENT CAMPS
   Santa Fe, N. Mex.
   Bismarck, N. Dak.
   Crystal City, Tex.
   Missoula, Mont.

△ CITIZEN ISOLATION CAMPS
   Moab, Utah ·
   Leupp, Ariz.

Map from *Years of Infamy: The Untold Story of America's Concentration Camps*. Rev. Ed., by Michi Nishiura Weglyn, University of Washington Press. Used by permission.

Island and Tuna Canyon (California), Kenedy Internment Center (Texas), Camp McCoy (Wisconsin), Camp Lordsburg and Fort Stanton (New Mexico), Kooskia Work Camp (Idaho), Fort Lincoln (North Dakota), Leavenworth Federal Penitentiary (Kansas), McNeil Island Federal Penitentiary (Washington), Fort Sill and Stringtown (Oklahoma); and sites in Hawaii, such as Sand Island and Honouliuli (Oahu), Kalaheo stockade (Kauai), and the Haiku camp (Maui).

EXECUTIVE ORDER

- - - - - - -

AUTHORIZING THE SECRETARY OF WAR TO PRESCRIBE
MILITARY AREAS

WHEREAS the successful prosecution of the war

requires every possible protection against espionage

and against sabotage to national-defense material,

national-defense premises, and national-defense util-

ities as defined in Section 4, Act of April 20, 1918,

40 Stat. 533, as amended by the Act of November 30,

1940, 54 Stat. 1220, and the Act of August 21, 1941,

55 Stat. 655 (U. S. C., Title 50, Sec. 104):

NOW, THEREFORE, by virtue of the authority

vested in me as President of the United States, and

Commander in Chief of the Army and Navy, I hereby

authorize and direct the Secretary of War, and the

Military Commanders whom he may from time to time

designate, whenever he or any designated Commander

deems such action necessary or desirable, to prescribe

military areas in such places and of such extent as he

or the appropriate Military Commander may determine,

from which any or all persons may be excluded, and with

respect to which, the right of any person to enter, re-

main in, or leave shall be subject to whatever restric-

tions the Secretary of War or the appropriate Military

Executive Order 9066
National Archives

Commander may impose in his discretion. The Secretary of War is hereby authorized to provide for residents of any such area who are excluded therefrom, such transportation, food, shelter, and other accommodations as may be necessary, in the judgment of the Secretary of War or the said Military Commander, and until other arrangements are made, to accomplish the purpose of this order. The designation of military areas in any region or locality shall supersede designations of prohibited and restricted areas by the Attorney General under the Proclamations of December 7 and 8, 1941, and shall supersede the responsibility and authority of the Attorney General under the said Proclamations in respect of such prohibited and restricted areas.

I hereby further authorize and direct the Secretary of War and the said Military Commanders to take such other steps as he or the appropriate Military Commander may deem advisable to enforce compliance with the restrictions applicable to each Military area hereinabove authorized to be designated, including the use of Federal troops and other Federal Agencies, with authority to accept assistance of state and local agencies.

Executive Order 9066 (continued)
National Archives

I hereby further authorize and direct all Executive Departments, independent establishments and other Federal Agencies, to assist the Secretary of War or the said Military Commanders in carrying out this Executive Order, including the furnishing of medical aid, hospitalization, food, clothing, transportation, use of land, shelter, and other supplies, equipment, utilities, facilities, and services.

This order shall not be construed as modifying or limiting in any way the authority heretofore granted under Executive Order No. 8972, dated December 12, 1941, nor shall it be construed as limiting or modifying the duty and responsibility of the Federal Bureau of Investigation, with respect to the investigation of alleged acts of sabotage or the duty and responsibility of the Attorney General and the Department of Justice under the Proclamations of December 7 and 8, 1941, prescribing regulations for the conduct and control of alien enemies, except as such duty and responsibility is superseded by the designation of military areas hereunder.

THE WHITE HOUSE,

February /4, 1942.

Frankl- D pesurch

FEB 21 12 51 PM '42

FEDERAL REGISTER

Executive Order 9066 (continued)
National Archives

C. E. Order 108

**WESTERN DEFENSE COMMAND AND FOURTH ARMY
WARTIME CIVIL CONTROL ADMINISTRATION**
Presidio of San Francisco, California

INSTRUCTIONS
TO ALL PERSONS OF
JAPANESE
ANCESTRY
LIVING IN THE FOLLOWING AREA:

All that portion of the County of Tulare, State of California, within the boundary beginning at the point at which the westerly line of U. S. Highway No. 99 intersects the Fresno-Tulare County Line; thence northeasterly along said County Line to its intersection with the westerly line of California State Highway No. 65; thence southerly along the westerly line of said Highway No. 65 to its intersection with California State Highway No. 198; thence westerly along the southerly line of said State Highway No. 198 to its intersection with U. S. Highway No. 99; thence northwesterly along the westerly line of said Highway No. 99 to the point of beginning.

Pursuant to the provisions of Civilian Exclusion Order No. 108, this Headquarters, dated July 22, 1942, all persons of Japanese ancestry, both alien and non-alien, will be evacuated from the above area by 12 o'clock noon, P.W.T., Tuesday, August 11, 1942.

No Japanese person will be permitted to move into, or out of, the above area after 5:00 A. M., P.W.T., Wednesday, July 22, 1942, without obtaining special permission from the representative of the Commanding General, Northern California Sector, at the Civil Control Station located at:

Visalia Municipal Auditorium,
Visalia, California.

Such permits will only be granted for the purpose of uniting members of a family, or in cases of grave emergency.

The Civil Control Station is equipped to assist the Japanese population affected by this evacuation in the following ways:

1. Give advice and instructions on the evacuation.

2. Provide services with respect to the management, leasing, sale, storage or other disposition of most kinds of property, such as real estate, business and professional equipment, household goods, boats, automobiles and livestock.

Instructions to implement Civilian Exclusion Order No. 108
National Archives

3. Provide temporary   ,idence elsewhere for all Japanese in family groups.

4. Transport persons and a limited amount of clothing and equipment to their new residence.

THE FOLLOWING INSTRUCTIONS MUST BE OBSERVED:

1. A responsible member of each family, preferably the head of the family, or the person in whose name most of the property is held, and each individual living alone, will report to the Civil Control Station to receive further instructions. This must be done between 8:00 A. M. and 5:00 P. M. on Monday, July 27, 1942, or between 8:00 A. M. and 5:00 P. M. on Tuesday, July 28, 1942.

2. Evacuees must carry with them on departure for the Relocation Project the following property:

  (a) Bedding and linens (no mattress) for each member of the family;
  (b) Toilet articles for each member of the family;
  (c) Extra clothing for each member of the family;
  (d) Essential personal effects for each member of the family, provided the total baggage does not exceed 150 pounds for each person over 11 years of age and 75 pounds for each child under 12 and over 5 years of age. Other personal effects can be shipped at the evacuees' expense, by parcel post or express to the Relocation Project.

All items taken on the train or shipped must be packaged, tied and plainly marked with the name of the owner and numbered according to instructions obtained at the Civil Control Station where more detailed information can be obtained as to items likely to be needed.

3. No pets of any kind will be permitted.

4. The United States Government through its agencies will provide for the storage, at the sole risk of the owner, of the more substantial household items, such as iceboxes, washing machines, pianos and other heavy furniture. Cooking utensils and other small items will be accepted for storage if crated, packed and plainly marked with the name and address of the owner. Only one name and address will be used by a given family.

5. Each family, and individual living alone, will be furnished transportation to the Relocation Project. Private means of transportation will not be utilized. All instructions pertaining to the movement will be obtained at the Civil Control Station.

Go to the Civil Control Station between the hours of 8:00 A. M. and 5:00 P. M., Monday, July 27, 1942, or between the hours of 8:00 A. M. and 5:00 P. M., Tuesday, July 28, 1942, to receive further instructions.

J. L. DeWitt
Lieutenant General, U. S. Army
Commanding

July 22, 1942

See Civilian Exclusion Order No. 108.

Instructions to implement Civilian Exclusion Order No. 108 (continued)
National Archives

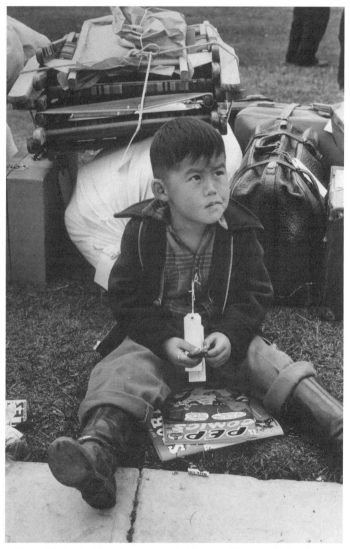

Salinas, California. Tagged for removal. *Library of Congress Prints & Photographs Division Washington, DC, LC-USF34-072499-D*

Okano Brothers five and dime store prepares for evacuation, San Francisco 1942. *Courtesy National Archives, ARC Identifier 195537*

Woodland, California, families at railroad station awaiting relocation to the Merced Assembly Center, May 20, 1942. *Courtesy National Archives, ARC Identifier 537804*

Los Angeles County, California. The mass removal of Japanese and
Japanese-Americans from West coast areas under United States Army
war emergency order. Japanese arrive at the Santa Anita reception center.
*Library of Congress Prints & Photographs Division Washington, DC,
LC-USF34-072312-D*

Santa Anita reception center, Los Angeles County, California. The
exclusion of Japanese and Japanese-Americans from West coast areas
under United States Army war emergency order. Examining baggage of
Japanese as they arrive. *Library of Congress Prints & Photographs Division
Washington, DC, LC-USF34-072331-D*

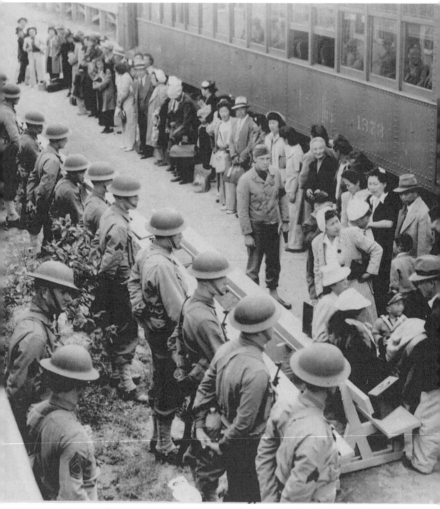

Persons of Japanese ancestry arrive at the Santa Anita Assembly Center from San Pedro. Incarcerees lived at this center at the former Santa Anita race track before being moved inland to permanent concentration camps. *Courtesy National Archives, ARC Identifier 537040*

Photograph of Dust Storm at Manzanar War Relocation Authority Center: 07/03/1942. *Courtesy National Archives, ARC Identifier 539960*

Santa Anita reception center, Los Angeles County, California. The expulsion of Japanese and Japanese Americans from West coast areas under United States Army war emergency order. Japanese family eating their first meal at the center. *Library of Congress Prints & Photographs Division Washington, DC, LC-USF34-072348-D*

NOTE ON TERMINOLOGY

This interpretive essay uses terminology that describes what federal and state government actually did to more than 110,000 persons of Japanese ancestry, the vast majority of whom were U.S. citizens. Confusion, ignorance, and controversy attend the question of terminology for the mass removal and imprisonment of Nikkei during World War II. President Roosevelt and high officials used the term "concentration camps" for the mass imprisonment of Japanese aliens and U.S. citizens alike, but bureaucrats created and popularized a clever vocabulary of euphemisms to obscure what was really going on in the vast gulag of concentration camps for political prisoners who had been judged guilty solely by reason of their race. "Non-aliens" was an insidiously innocuous euphemism for U.S. citizens denied their basic civil rights. Words such as "evacuation" and "relocation" were intended to mask official policies that today we would describe as "ethnic cleansing."

For a more detailed review of the need for a more accurate nomenclature on the subject, readers are directed to the following essays available at the National Park Service Web site on Tule Lake (http://www.nps.gov/tule/): Roger Daniels, *Words Do Matter: A Note on Inappropriate Terminology and the Incarceration of Japanese Americans*; Aiko Herzig-Yoshinaga, *Words Can Lie or Clarify: Terminology of the World War II Incarceration of Japanese Americans*; James Hirabayashi, *"Concentration Camp" or "Relocation Center"—What's In A Name?*: Japanese American Citizens League, *National Resolution on Preferred Terminology*; Mako Nakagawa, *The Power of Words*; and Raymond Okamura, *The American Concentration Camps: A Cover-Up through Euphemistic Terminology.*

Selected Bibliography

Scholarly and popular accounts of the World War II incarceration of Nikkei are extensive and available in print, documentary films and videos, Web sites, and on the Internet. Readers are cautioned that the available materials vary greatly in their historical accuracy and perspectives. The following selection of recommended titles begins with general works on Japanese American history, including the arrival and settlement of Japanese in North America and other parts of the Western Hemisphere prior to World War II. The second category of titles reflects multidisciplinal scholarly studies of the wartime Nikkei gulag and diaspora, as well as autobiographical accounts. Most of these titles balance the voluminous apologist literature that portrays WRA activities as an exercise in benevolence, as in the U.S. Department of the Interior's *WRA, A Story of Human Conservation* (Washington, D.C., 1946). Postwar recovery and the Redress Movement comprise a third broad category. The final sections suggest key titles in the rapidly expanding range of multimedia documentaries on film, video, Web sites, and the Internet.

General Works on
Japanese American History

Asian Women United of California. *Making Waves: An Anthology of Writings By and About Asian American Women* (Boston, 1989). Valerie Matsumoto and Gail Nomura contribute historical pieces on Nikkei women.

Azuma, Eiichiro. *Between Two Empires: Race, History, and Transnationalism in Japanese America* (New York, 2005).

Chan, Sucheng. *Asian Americans: An Interpretive History* (Boston, 1991).

Chuman, Frank F. *The Bamboo People: The Law and Japanese Americans* (Del Mar, CA, 1976).

Daniels, Roger. *The Politics of Prejudice: The Anti-Japanese Movement in California and the Struggle for Japanese Exclusion* (Berkeley, 1962).

Gardiner, C. Harvey. *The Japanese and Peru, 1873–1973* (Albuquerque, NM, 1975)

Glenn, Evelyn Nakano. *Issei, Nisei, Warbride: Three Generations of Japanese American Women in Domestic Service* (Philadelphia, 1986).

Hane, Mikiso. *Peasants, Rebels and Outcastes; The Underside of Modern Japan* (New York, 1982). Burdens imposed on rural regions by modernization during the Meiji era caused an exodus of emigrants who became Issei or first-generation immigrant pioneers throughout the Western Hemisphere.

Hata, Donald Teruo. *"Undesirables:" Early Immigrants and the Anti-Japanese Movement in San Francisco, 1892–1893* (New York, 1978).

Hayashi, Brian Masaru. *'For the Sake of Our Japanese Brethren:' Assimilation, Nationalism, and Protestantism Among the Japanese of Los Angeles, 1895–1942* (Stanford, 1995).

Hirabayashi, Lane Ryo, Akemi Kikumura-Yano, and James A. Hirabayashi. *New Worlds, New Lives: Globalization and People of Japanese Descent in the Americas and from Latin America in Japan* (Stanford, 2002).

Hirahara, Naomi. *An American Son: The Story of George Aratani, Founder of Mikasa and Kenwood* (Los Angeles, 2001).

——, ed. *Greenmakers: Japanese American Gardeners in Southern California* (Los Angeles, 2000).

Hosokawa, Bill. *Nisei: The Quiet Americans* (New York, 1969).

Ichioka, Yuji. *The Issei: The World of the First Generation Japanese Immigrants, 1885–1924* (New York, 1988).

——, Yasuo Sakata, Nobuya Tsuchida, and Eri Yasuhara, eds. *A Buried Past: An Annotated Bibliography of the Japanese American Research Project Collection* [UCLA] (Los Angeles, 1974).

——, and Eiichiro Azuma, eds. *A Buried Past II: A Sequel to the Annotated Bibliography of the Japanese American Research Project Collection* [UCLA] (Los Angeles, 1999).

Ito, Kazuo. *Issei: A History of Japanese Immigrants in North America.* Translated by Shinichiro Nakamura and Jean S. Gerard (Seattle, 1973).

Iwata, Masakazu. *Planted In Good Soil: A History of the Issei in United States Agriculture* (New York, 1992).

Kessler, Lauren. *Stubborn Twig: Three Generations in the Life of a Japanese American Family* (New York, 1993).

Kikumura, Akemi. *Through Harsh Winters: The Life of a Japanese Immigrant Woman* (Novato, CA, 1981). Biography of the author's mother.

——. *Promises Kept: The Life of an Issei Man* (Novato, CA, 1991). Biography of the author's father.

Kikumura-Yano, Akemi, ed. *Encyclopedia of Japanese Descendants in the Americas: An Illustrated History of the Nikkei* (New York, 2002).

Kitano, Harry H. L. *Japanese Americans: The Evolution of a Subculture* (Englewood Cliffs, NJ, 1969).

——. *Generations and Identity: The Japanese American* (Needham, Mass, 1993).

Kochiyama, Yuri Nakahara. *Passing It On—A Memoir* (Los Angeles, 2004).

Kurashige, Lon. *Japanese American Celebration and Conflict: A History of Ethnic Identity and Festival in Los Angeles, 1934–1990* (Berkeley, 2002).

Matsumoto, Valerie J. *Farming the Home Place: A Japanese American Community in California, 1919–1982* (Ithaca, NY, 1993).

Nakano, Mei T. *Japanese American Women: Three Generations 1890–1990* (San Francisco, 1990).

Nakasone, Ronald Y., ed. *Okinawan Diaspora* (Honolulu, 2002).

Niiya, Brian, ed. *Japanese American History: An A-to-Z Reference from 1868 to the Present* (New York, 1991).

Odo, Franklin, ed. *The Columbia Documentary History of the Asian American Experience* (New York, 2002).

Okihiro, Gary Y. *Cane Fires: The Anti-Japanese Movement in Hawaii, 1865–1945* (Philadelphia, 1991).

——. *The Columbia Guide to Asian American History* (New York, 2005).

Shaw Historical Library. "A Question of Loyalty: Internment at Tule Lake," *The Journal of the Shaw Historical Library at the Oregon Institute of Technology* (Volume 19, 2005).

Spickard, Paul R. *Japanese Americans: The Formation and Transformation of an Ethnic Group* (New York, 1996).

Takaki, Ronald. *Pau Hana: Plantation Life and Labor in Hawaii, 1835–1920* (Honolulu, 1983).

——. *Strangers from a Different Shore: A History of Asian Americans* (New York, 1989).

Uyeda, Clifford L. *Suspended: Growing Up Asian in America* (San Francisco, 2000).

Wilson, Robert A., and Bill Hosokawa. *East To America: A History of the Japanese in the United States* (New York, 1980).

THE WORLD WAR II INCARCERATION
OF JAPANESE AMERICANS

Adachi, Ken. *The Enemy That Never Was: A History of the Japanese* Canadians (Toronto, 1976).

Adams, Ansel. *Born Free and Equal: The Story of Loyal Japanese Americans at Manzanar Relocation Center, Inyo County, California* (New York, 1944).

Akashi, Motomu. *Betrayed Trust: The Story of a Deported Issei and His American-born Family During World War II* (Bloomington, IN, 2004).

Bahr, Diana Meyers. *The Unquiet Nisei: An Oral History of the Life of Sue Kunitomi Embrey* (New York, 2007).

Bailey, Paul. *City in the Sun: The Japanese Concentration Camp at Poston, Arizona* (Los Angeles, 1971).

Bosworth, Alan R. *America's Concentration Camps* (New York, 1967).

Broom (Bloom), Leonard, and Ruth Riemer. *Removal and Return: The Socio-Economic Effects of the War on Japanese Americans* (Berkeley, 1949).

Burton, Jeffrey F., et al. *Three Farewells to Manzanar: The Archeology of Manzanar National Historic Site, California* (Tucson, AZ, 1996).

——. *Confinement and Ethnicity: An Overview of World War II Japanese American Relocation Sites* (Tucson, AZ, 1999).

——. *I REI TO: Archeological Investigations at the Manzanar Relocation Center Cemetery, Manzanar National Historic Site, California* (Tucson, AZ, 2001).

Castelnuovo, Shirley. *Soldiers of Conscience: Japanese American Military Resisters in World War II* (Westport, CT, 2008).

Christgau, John. "Collins versus the World: The Fight to Restore Citizenship to Japanese American Renunciants of World War II," *Pacific Historical Review* (Vol. LIV, No. 1, February, 1985): 1–31.

Collins, Donald E. *Native American Aliens: Disloyalty and the Renunciation of Citizenship by Japanese Americans during World War II* (Westport, CT, 1985). On Tule

Lake's role as the only Segregation Center among the WRA concentration camps.

Conrat, Maisie and Richard. *Executive Order 9066: The Internment of 110,000 Japanese Americans* (San Francisco, 1972; Los Angeles, 1992).

Corbett, Scott. *Quiet Passages: The Exchange of Civilians between the United States and Japan during the Second World War* (Kent, OH, 1987).

Crost, Lyn. *Honor by Fire: Japanese Americans at War in Europe and the Pacific* (Novato, CA, 1994).

Daniels, Roger. *The Decision to Relocate the Japanese Americans* (New York, 1975).

——. *Concentration Camps North America: Japanese in the United States and Canada during World War II* (Malibar, FL, 1981).

——. *Prisoners Without Trial: Japanese Americans and World War II* (New York, 1993).

——. *Words Do Matter: A Note on Inappropriate Terminology and the Incarceration of Japanese Americans* (Seattle, 2005); also appears as an article in Louis Fiset and Gail Nomura, eds., *Nikkei in the Pacific Northwest: Japanese Americans and Japanese Canadians in the Twentieth Century* (Seattle, 2005).

Dempster, Brian Komei, ed. *From Our Side of the Fence: Growing Up in America's Concentration Camps* (San Francisco, 2001).

de Nevers, Klancy Clark. *The Colonel and the Pacifist: Karl Bendetsen, Perry Saito and the Incarceration of Japanese Americans during World War II* (Salt Lake City, 2004).

de Queiroz, Chizuko Judy Sugita. *Camp Days, 1942–1945* (Irvine, CA, 2004). Watercolor illustrations of daily life in the Colorado River concentration camp at Poston, AZ.

Dower, John. *War Without Mercy: Race & Power in the Pacific War* (New York, 1986).

Drinnon, Richard. *Keeper of Concentration Camps: Dillon S. Myer and American Racism* (Berkeley, 1987).

Duus, Masayo Umezawa. *Unlikely Liberators: The Men of the 100th and the 442nd* (Honolulu, 1987).

Eaton, Allen Hendershott. *Beauty Behind Barbed Wire: The Arts of the Japanese in Our War Relocation Camps* (New York, 1952).

Embrey, Sue Kunitomi, Arthur A. Hansen, and Betty K. Mitson. *Manzanar Martyr: An Interview with Harry Y. Ueno* (Fullerton, CA, 1986).

Fiset, Louis. *Imprisoned Apart: The World War II Correspondence of an Issei Couple* (Seattle, 1997).

——, and Gail M. Nomura, eds. *Nikkei in the Pacific Northwest: Japanese Americans and Japanese Canadians in the Twentieth Century* (Seattle, 2005).

Fukuda, Rev. Yoshiaki. *My Six Years of Internment: An Issei's Struggle for Justice* (San Francisco, 1990).

Gardiner, Harvey C. *Pawns in a Triangle of Hate: The Peruvian Japanese and the United States* (Seattle, 1981).

Garrett, Jessie A., and Ronald C. Larson. *Camp and Community: Manzanar and the Owens Valley* (Fullerton, 1977).

Gesensway, Deborah, and Mindy Roseman. *Beyond Words: Images from America's Concentration Camps* (Ithaca, NY, 1987).

Girdner, Audrie, and Anne Loftis. *The Great Betrayal: The Evacuation of Japanese-Americans during World War II* (New York, 1969).

Gordon, Linda, and Gary Y. Okihiro, eds. *Impounded: Dorothea Lange and the Censored Images of Japanese American Internment* (New York, 2006).

Grodzins, Morton. *The Loyal and The Disloyal* (Chicago, 1956).

——. *Americans Betrayed: Politics of the Japanese American Evacuation* (Chicago, 1949).

Hansen, Arthur, and Betty E. Mitson, eds. *Voices Long Silent: An Oral Inquiry into the Japanese American Evacuation* (Fullerton, CA, 1974).

Harth, Erica, ed. *Last Witnesses: Reflections on the Wartime Internment of Japanese Americans* (New York, 2001).

Hayashi, Brian Masaru. *Democratizing the Enemy: The Japanese American Internment* (Princeton, NJ, 2008).

Herzig-Yoshinaga, Aiko. *Words Can Lie or Clarify: Terminology of the World War II Incarceration of Japanese Americans* (Torrance, CA, 2010).

Higashide, Seiichi. *Adios to Tears: The Memoirs of a Japanese-Peruvian Internee in U.S. Concentration Camps* (Honolulu, 1993; Seattle, 2000).

Hill, Kimi Kodani. *Topaz Moon: Chiura Obata's Art of the Internment* (Berkeley, 2000).

Hirabayashi, James. "'Concentration Camp' or 'Relocation Center'—What's In A Name?" *Japanese American National Museum Quarterly* (Los Angeles, 1994).

Hirabayashi, Lane. *Inside An American Concentration Camp: Japanese American Resistance at Poston, Arizona* (Tucson, 1995).

——. *The Politics of Fieldwork: Research in an American Concentration Camp* (Tucson, 1999). On the practices of Japanese American Evacuation and Resettlement Study staff.

——, with Kenichiro Shimada. *Japanese American Resettlement Through the Lens: Hikaru Carl Iwasaki and the WRA's Photographic Section, 1943–1945* (Boulder, CO, 2009).

Hirahara, Naomi, and Gwenn M. Jensen. *Silent Scars of Healing Hands: Oral Histories of Japanese American Doctors in World War II Detention Camps* (Fullerton, CA, 2004).

Hohri, William Minoru, et al. *Resistance: Challenging America's Wartime Internment of Japanese-Americans* (Kearney, NE, 2001).

Houston, Jeanne Wakatsuki. *Farewell to Manzanar* (Boston, 1973). Autobiographical.

Ichioka, Yuji, ed. *Views from Within: The Japanese American Evacuation and Resettlement Study* (Los Angeles, 1989).

Inada, Lawson, ed. *Only What We Could Carry: The Japanese American Internment Experience* (Berkeley, 2000).

Inouye, Daniel. *Journey to Washington* (Englewood Cliffs, NJ, 1967).

Irons, Peter. *Justice at War: The Story of the Japanese American Internment Cases* (New York, 1983).

——, ed. *Justice Delayed: The Record of the Japanese American Internment Cases* (Middletown, CT, 1989).

Irwin, Catherine. *Twice Orphaned: Voices from the Children's Village at Manzanar* (Fullerton, 2008).

Ishigo, Estelle. *Lone Heart Mountain* (Los Angeles, 1972). Line drawings and text by the artist, who is the subject of Steven Okazaki's film, *Days of Waiting*.

Ishizuka, Karen. *Lost and Found: Reclaiming the Japanese American Incarceration* (Chicago, 2006).

James, Thomas. *Exile Within: The Schooling of Japanese Americans, 1942–1945* (Cambridge, 1987).

Japanese American Historical Society of Southern California. *Nanka Nikkei Voices* (Torrance, CA, 1998, 2002, 2004). Minimally edited, brief autobiographical statements.

Kashima, Tetsuden. *Judgment Without Trial: Japanese American Imprisonment during World War II* (Seattle, 2003).

Kikuchi, Charles. Edited and with an introduction by John Modell, *The Kikuchi Diary: Chronicle from an American Concentration Camp* (Urbana, IL, 1973).

Kitagawa, Daisuke. *Issei and Nisei: The Internment Years* (New York, 1967).

Kiyota, Minoru. Translated from Japanese by Linda Klepinger Keenan. *Beyond Loyalty: The Story of a Kibei* (Honolulu, 1997).

Kohlhoff, Dean. *When the Wind Was a River: Aleut Evacuation in World War II* (Seattle, 1995).

Kumei, Teruko Imai. "Skeleton in the Closet: The Japanese American Hokoku Seinen-dan and Their 'Disloyal' Activities at the Tule Lake Segregation Center during World War II," *The Japanese Journal of American Studies* (No.7, 1996): 67–102.

Leighton, Alexander H. *The Governing of Men: General Principles and Recommendations Based on the Experience at a Japanese Relocation Camp* (Princeton, NJ, 1945).

Lim, Deborah K. *The Lim Report: A Research Project of Japanese Americans in America's Concentration Camps during World War II* (Kearney, NE, 1990, 2002). Original, complete version of the report on the investigation commissioned by the JACL into allegations about its self-serving wartime relations with the WRA.

Mackey, Mike, ed. *Remembering Heart Mountain: Essays on Japanese American Internment in Wyoming* (Casper, WY, 1998).

——, ed. *Guilt by Association: Essays on Japanese Settlement, Internment, and Relocation in the Rocky Mountain West* (Powell, WY, 2001).

Masaoka, Mike, with Bill Hosokawa. *They Call Me Moses Masaoka* (New York, 1987).

Masuda, Minoru. Edited by Hana Masuda and Dianne Bridgman. *Letters from the 442nd: The World War II*

Correspondence of a Japanese American Medic (Seattle, 2008).

Matsuoka, Jack. *Poston: Camp 11, Block 211* (San Francisco, 1974). A cartoonist's view of daily life in the Colorado River concentration camp.

Miyakawa, Edward T. *Tule Lake* (Victoria, B.C., Canada, 2002).

Muller, Eric L. *Free to Die for Their Country: The True Story of the Japanese American Draft Resisters in World War II* (Chicago, 2001).

——. *American Inquisition: The Hunt for Japanese American Disloyalty in World War II* (Chapel Hill, NC, 2007).

Murphy, Thomas D. *Ambassadors In Arms: The Story of Hawaii's 100th Battalion* (Honolulu, 1955).

Murray, Alice Yang. *What Did the Internment of Japanese Americans Mean?* (Boston, 2000).

Myer, Dillon. *Uprooted Americans: The Japanese Americans and the War Relocation Authority during World War II* (Tucson, AZ, 1971).

Nagata, Donna K. *Legacy of Injustice: Exploring the Cross-Generational Impact of the Japanese American Internment* (New York, 1993).

Nakagawa, Mako. *The Power of Words* (Seattle, 2009).

Nakagawa, Martha. *Renunciants: Bill Nishimura and Tad Yamakido* (Gardena, CA, 2005).

Nakamura, Toshiko Eto. *Nurse of Manzanar* (Bellingham, WA, 2008).

Nakanishi, Don T., ed. "The Japanese American Internment: Commemorative Issue," *Amerasia Journal* (19:1,1993).

National Archives and Records Administration, American Historical Association, Community College Humanities Association, and the Organization of American Historians, *Internment of Japanese Americans: Documents from the National Archives* (Dubuque, IA, 1990).

National Japanese American Historical Society. *Due Process: Americans of Japanese Ancestry and the United States Constitution, 1787–1994* (San Francisco, 1995). Documents, photographs, and chronology.

Nelson, Douglas W. *Heart Mountain: The History of an American Concentration Camp* (Madison, WI, 1976).

Ng, Wendy. *Japanese Internment during World War II: A History and Reference Guide* (Westport, CT, 2002).

Nishimoto, Richard S. *Inside an American Concentration Camp: Japanese American Resistance at Poston, Arizona* (Tucson, AZ, 1995).

Odo, Franklin, ed. *No Sword to Bury: Japanese Americans in Hawaii during World War II* (Philadelphia, 2004).

Okada, John. *No-No Boy* (Rutherford, VT, 1957; reprinted Seattle, 1979). Novel about the consequences of negative replies to the loyalty questionnaire.

Okamura, Raymond. "The American Concentration Camps: A Cover-Up through Euphemistic Terminology," *The Journal of Ethnic Studies* (X:3, 1982).

Okihiro, Gary Y. *Storied Lives: Japanese American Students and World War II* (Seattle, 1999).

——. *Whispered Silences: Japanese Americans and World War II* (Seattle, 1996).

Okubo, Mine. *Citizen 13660* (New York, 1946). Autobiographical, illustrations and narrative by artist Okubo, based on her incarceration at Tanforan and Topaz.

Oppenheim, Joanne. *Dear Miss Breed: True Stories of the Japanese American Incarceration during World War II and a Librarian Who Made a Difference* (New York, 2006). The story of Clara Breed, children's librarian at the San Diego Public Library.

Robinson, Gerald H. *Elusive Truth: Four Photographers at Manzanar* (Nevada City, CA, 2002). Photos by Ansel Adams, Dorothea Lange, Clem Albers, and Toyo Miyatake.

Robinson, Greg. *By Order of the President: FDR and the Internment of Japanese Americans* (Cambridge, MA, 2001).

——. and Elena Tajima Cleef, eds. *Mine Okubo: Following Her Own Road* (Seattle, 2008).

——. *Tragedy of Democracy: Japanese Confinement in North America* (New York, 2009).

Sato, Kiyo. *Kiyo's Story: A Japanese American Family's Quest for the American Dream* (New York, 2009). Originally published as *Dandelion Through the Cracks,* autobiographical, former inmate of Poston, rejected by several nursing schools but rose to rank of captain in the Army Nursing Corps.

Saunders, Kay, and Roger Daniels, eds. *Alien Justice: Wartime Internment in Australia and North America* (Queensland, Australia, 2000).

Seigal, Shizue. *In Good Conscience: Supporting Japanese Americans during the Internment* (San Mateo, CA, 2006). The unsung efforts of individuals and organizations like the Quakers.

Shibutani, Tamotsu. *The Derelicts of Company K: A Sociological Study of Demoralization* (Berkeley, 1978).

Shimomura, Roger. *Minidoka On My Mind: Recent Work by Roger Shimomura* (Kansas City, KS, 2008).

Shirai, Noboru. *Tule Lake: An Issei Memoir* (Sacramento, CA, 2001).

Soga, Yasutaro. *Life Behind Barbed Wire: The World War II Internment Memoirs of a Hawaii Issei* (Honolulu, 2008).

Sone, Monica. *Nisei Daughter* (Seattle, 1953). Autobiographical, born in Seattle, inmate at Minidoka.

Spicer, Edward H., et al., *Impounded People: Japanese Americans in the Relocation Centers* (Tucson, AZ, 1969).

Takei, Barbara. *Legalizing Detention: Segregated Japanese Americans and the Justice Department's Renunciation Program* (Sacramento, CA, 2005).

———, and Judy Tachibana. *Tule Lake Revisited: A Brief Guide to the Tule Lake Internment Camp Site* (Sacramento, CA, 2001).

Takemoto, Paul Howard. *Nisei Memories: My Parents Talk About the War Years* (Seattle, 2006).

Tateishi, John. *And Justice For All: An Oral History of the Japanese American Detention Camps* (New York, 1984).

Taylor, Sandra C. *Jewel of the Desert: Japanese American Internment at Topaz* (Berkeley, 1993).

tenBroek, Jacobus, Edward N. Barnhart, and Floyd W. Matson. *Prejudice, War and the Constitution: Causes and Consequences of the Evacuation of the Japanese Americans in World War II* (Berkeley, 1954).

Thomas, Dorothy S. *The Salvage* (Berkeley, 1952). Second published report (see *The Spoilage*) of the Japanese American Evacuation and Resettlement Study (JERS).

———, and Richard Nishimoto. *The Spoilage: Japanese American Evacuation and Resettlement During World War II* (Berkeley, 1946).

Tomita, Mary Kimoto. *Dear Miye: Letters Home from Japan, 1939–1946* (Stanford, 1995).

Tule Lake Committee, John R. Ross and Reiko Ross. *Second Kinenhi: Reflections on Tule Lake* (San Francisco, CA, 2000).

Uchida, Yoshiko. *Journey to Topaz* (New York, 1971).

Weglyn, Michi Nishiura. *Years of Infamy: The Untold Story of America's Concentration Camps* (New York, 1976).

Woodward, Mary. *In Defense of Our Neighbors: The Walt and Milly Woodward Story* (Bainbridge Isle, WA, 2008).

Yoo, David K. *Growing Up Nisei: Race, Generation, and Culture among Japanese Americans of California, 1924–49* (Urbana, IL, 2000).

Postwar Recovery
and the Redress Movement

Bannai, Lorraine K. *Taking the Stand: The Lessons of Three Men Who Took the Japanese Internment to Court* (Seattle, 2005).

Commission on Wartime Relocation and Internment of Civilians, *Personal Justice Denied: Report of the Commission on Wartime Relocation and Internment of Civilians* (Washington, D.C., 1982); the University of Washington Press reprint (Seattle, 1997), includes a Foreword by Tetsuden Kashima and the *CWRIC's "Part 2 Recommendations"* (thirteen-page follow-up to its main report of December 1982 that was issued as a separate publication in June of 1983).

Daniels, Roger, Sandra C. Taylor, and Harry H. L. Kitano, eds. *Japanese Americans: From Relocation to Redress*, Revised Edition (Seattle, 1991).

Fujita-Rony, Thomas F. " 'Destructive Force:' Aiko Herzig-Yoshinaga's Gendered Labor in the Japanese-American Redress Movement," *Frontiers: A Journal of Women's Studies* (24:1, 2003).

Hatayama, Leslie T. *Righting a Wrong: Japanese Americans and the Passage of the Civil Liberties Act of 1988* (Stanford, CA, 1993).

Hohri, William. *Repairing America: An Account of the Movement for Japanese-American Redress* (Pullman, WA, 1988).

Iijima, Chris. *Reparations and the 'Model Minority' Ideology of Acquiescence: The Necessity to Refute the Return to Original Humiliation* (Boston,1998).

Maki, Mitchell T., Harry H.L. Kitano, and S. Megan Berthold. *Achieving the Impossible Dream: How Japanese Americans Obtained Redress* (Urbana, IL, 1999).

Murray, Alice Yang. *Historical Memories of the Japanese American Internment and the Struggle for Redress* (Stanford, 2008).

Shimabukuro, Robert S. *Born In Seattle: The Campaign for Japanese American Redress* (Seattle, 2001).

Sogi, Francis Y., and Yeiichi (Kelly) Kuwayama. *Japanese Americans Disunited: How a memorial to unify the Japanese American community became a symbol of disunity* (Washington, D.C., 2001).

Takezawa, Yasuko I. *Breaking the Silence: Redress and Japanese American Ethnicity* (Ithaca, NY, 1995).

Yamamoto, Eric K., Margaret Chon, Carol L. Izumi, Jerry Kang, and Frank H. Wu. *Race, Rights, and Reparation: Law and the Japanese American Internment* (Gaithersburg, NY, 2001).

Films, Videos, and DVDs

Abe, Frank. *Conscience and the Constitution* (2000) examines the long-suppressed and still controversial story of Nisei "resisters of conscience" who opposed conscription while their families were imprisoned and denied their rights as U.S. citizens. 56 minutes.

Dexter, Don. *Camp Amache: The Story of An American Tragedy* (2007). 57 minutes.

Ding, Loni. *Color of Honor: The Japanese American Soldier in World War II* (1988). 90 minutes.

Fox, Joe, and James Nubile. *Passing Poston: An American Story* (2008). Former inmates like Ruth Okimoto confront childhood memories. 105 minutes.

Hattendorf, Linda. *The Cats of Mirikitani* (2008). Artist Jimmy Mirikitani's memories of the incarceration. 74 minutes.

Horsting, Robert, and Craig Yahata. *Citizen Tanouye* (2005). Torrance High School students research Medal of Honor recipient Ted Tanouye. 58 minutes.

Ina, Satsuki. *Children of the Camps* (1999). Psychological trauma persists among former incarcerees. 57 minutes.

———. *From a Silk Cocoon* (2006). A young couple's sad saga of separation and imprisonment during World War II. 57 minutes.

Ishizuka, Karen, and Bob Nakamura. *Toyo Miyatake: Infinite Shades of Gray* (2002). Photographer who smuggled a lens, constructed a camera, and recorded daily life at Manzanar concentration camp. 30 minutes.

Johnston, George. *Going For Honor, Going For Broke* (2006). Nisei soldiers. 16 minutes.

Kapitanoff, Nancy, and Sharon Yamato. *Out of Infamy: Michi Nishiura Weglyn* (2009). 17 minutes.

Kubota, Bill. *Most Honorable Son* (2007). Ben Kuroki who enlisted in the Army Air Corps and survived fifty-eight missions over Europe. 60 minutes.

Metzler, David. *The Lost Village of Terminal Island* (2007). Mass removal of Nikkei from this fishing village in the Port of Los Angeles. 42 minutes.

Nakamura, Tadashi. *A Song For Ourselves: A personal journey into the life and music of Asian American Movement troubadour Chris Iijima* (2009). 34 minutes.

National Park Service. *Remembering Manzanar: A Documentary* (2002). 22 minutes.

Okazaki, Steven. *Days of Waiting* (1988). Documentary on artist Estelle Ishigo, married to a Nisei and incarcerated at Heart Mountain. 28 minutes.

———. *Unfinished Business: The Japanese American Internment Cases* (1986). 58 minutes.

Omori, Emiko. *Rabbit in the Moon* (1999) interviews a diverse cast of former inmates and reveals social and political tensions, as well as resistance and collaboration. 85 minutes.

Pirosh, Robert. *Go For Broke* (1951). Commercial film, stars Van Johnson as a white officer assigned to the 442nd Regimental Combat Team. 92 minutes.

Tule Lake Committee and Anders Tomlinson. *My Face Was My Crime: Tule Lake Segregation Center* (2007). 32 minutes.

WEB SITES AND THE INTERNET

A comprehensive list of titles is updated at the Web site of the Center for Asian American Media (www.asianamericanmedia.org), formerly the National Asian American Telecommunications Association.

Civil Liberties and Public Education Fund (CLPEF). Established by the Civil Liberties Act of 1988: http://www.clpef.net

Densho, The Japanese American Legacy Project: www.densho.org

Discover Nikkei: www.discovernikkei.org

Go For Broke National Education Center: www.goforbroke.org

Hirasaki National Resource Center, Japanese American National Museum: www.janm.org/nrc

Japanese American Veterans Association: www.javadc.org

National Archives and Records Administration: www.nara.gov

National Japanese American Historical Society: www.njahs.org

National Park Service website on Manzanar: www.nps.gov/manz

National Park Service website on Tule Lake: www.nps.gov/tule/

University of Arkansas at Little Rock and the Japanese American National Museum in Los Angeles. Life Interrupted: The Japanese American Experience in World War II Arkansas: www.ualr.edu/lifeinterrupted/curriculum/index.asp

INDEX

National Museum of American
History, the Smithsonian, 55
National Origins Act, 9
National Park Service, 55–56
Native Sons of the Golden
West, 6
nativism, 6, 9
Nikkei (Japanese American),
1–3, 5, 8, 9, 13, 14, 17, 18, 25,
28, 31, 32, 39–43, 45, 47–48,
49–51, 54, 55, 56
Nisei (second generation), 1, 3,
9–12, 17, 23–24, 26, 28, 29,
32–33, 34, 36, 42, 43, 44, 45,
46, 48, 51, 56
Nisei, The Quiet Americans,
46
Nixon, Richard, 48
Noguchi, Thomas, 46

Obama, Barack, 2
Okamoto, Shoichi James, 28
Okamura, Raymond, 47
Olson, Culbert, 13
Omura, James, 18, 34
"outwhiting the whites," 43
Ozawa v. *United States*, 8

Pacific Coast Committee on
American Principles and Fair
Play, 39
Patel, Marilyn Hall, 54
Pearl Harbor, Hawaii, 12
Personal Justice Denied, 53
Peruvian Japanese, 2, 21
"picture brides," 6
Poston (*see* Colorado River
concentration camp), 19
Princeton University, 26

privacy, lack of in concentration
camps, 23
Puyallup (see Camp Harmony),
45

Quakers, 15, 25
"Question 27 and Question 28,"
28, 30
quotas on immigrants, 9

Reagan, Ronald, 2, 52, 55
"redress," 2, 48–49, 50, 55, 56
relocation centers, 20, 21, 22
restricted covenants, 10
Ridge, Martin, 44
Roberts Commission, 14
Rocky Shimpo, Denver, 34
Rohwer, Arkansas, 22
Roosevelt, Franklin D., 1, 13,
15–17, 21, 32
Roosevelt, Theodore, 6
Rostow, Eugene, 38
Russo-Japanese War, 7

San Francisco Board of
Education, 6
Sand Island, Hawaii, 17
Sansei (third generation), 43,
44, 45–46, 47, 51, 53
Santa Anita Assembly Center,
19–20, 26
Santa Fe, New Mexico, 22
Seagoville, Texas, 22
Selective Service Form 304A,
29–30
Schroeder, Mary, 54
September 11, 2001, 12–13
Shima, George, the "Potato
King," 6

Japanese Americans and World War II
Developmental and copyeditor: Andrew J. Davidson
Production editor: Linda Gaio
Interior design and typsetting: Bruce Leckie
Printer: McNaughton & Gunn, Inc.